Life With Our Father

The Better Life of Knowing God

By
James E. Laero

How blessed is God! And what a blessing he is! He's the Father of our Master, Jesus Christ, and takes us to the high places of blessing in him. Long before he laid down earth's foundations, he had us in mind, had settled on us as the focus of his love, to be made whole and holy by his love. Long, long ago he decided to adopt us into his family through Jesus Christ. (What pleasure he took in planning this!)
Ephesians 1:3-5 (the Message)

Life With Our Father
The Better Life of Knowing God
by James E. Laero

Copyright © 2011 James E. Laero

ISBN 978-1-61434-463-6

All rights reserved solely by the author. This book or parts thereof may not be reproduced in any form, stored in a retrieval system or transmitted in any form by any means - electronic, mechanical, photocopy, recording or otherwise - without prior written permission of the author, except as provided by United States of America copyright law.

Please note that much of this publication is based on personal experience. You should use this information as you see fit, and at your own risk. Your particular situation may not be exactly suited to the examples presented and you should adjust your use of the information and recommendations accordingly. Nothing in this publication is intended to replace common sense, legal, medical or other professional advice.

Published in the United States by Booklocker.com, Inc., Bangor, Maine.

Printed in the United States of America on acid-free paper.

Booklocker.com, Inc.
2011

First Edition

Scripture quotations marked KJV are from the King James Version of the Bible.

Scripture quotations marked NLT are taken from the Holy Bible, New Living Translation, copyright 1996, 2004. Used by permission of Tyndale House Publishers, Inc., Wheaton, Illinois 60189. All rights reserved.

Scripture taken from the HOLY BIBLE, NEW INTERNATIONAL VERSION®. Copyright © 1973, 1978, 1984 International Bible Society. Used by permission of Zondervan. All rights reserved. The "NIV" and "New International Version" trademarks are registered in the United States Patent and Trademark Office by International Bible Society. Use of either trademark requires the permission of International Bible Society.

"Scripture taken from the NEW AMERICAN STANDARD BIBLE®, Copyright © 1960,1962,1963,1968,1971,1972, 1973,1975,1977,1995 by The Lockman Foundation. Used by permission."

"Scripture taken from The Message. Copyright 1993, 1994, 1995, 1996, 2000, 2001, 2002. Used by permission of NavPress Publishing Group."

Life With Our Father

The Better Life Of Knowing God

Dedication

To my Lord Jesus, who by His Holy Spirit,
gently and faithfully brings me to a continuing
glorious revelation of my heavenly Father.

To my earthly family and my church family,
who by God's wonderful blessing are one, and are
they who epitomize the fatherhood of our Lord God
through their unwavering love to me.

And to you, the reader,
for your desire to know more about,
"Life With Our Father."

Acknowledgments

One of the great principles taught me by my heavenly Father is the understanding that we are truly all part of one another in Jesus Christ. Whatever we do and whatever we accomplish, is the result of many other people's lives being invested in ours. From the great writings of men and women of God gone to their rest, to my earthly parents and grandmother who always inspired me to seek Him. From the great men and women of the region where I live, to the heroes of my nation who place their lives on the line and who have given their lives that I may have the opportunity to worship my God in freedom. From my church family to my closest friends who inspire me each day to hold fast to my heavenly Father. The revelation, knowledge and understanding in this book granted to me by the Lord have come through countless people who touched my life. Each added a part to me, and in doing so have added the life of our heavenly Father to this book.

I wish to give them the honor that is due their love.

To all of you still here in body, and those gone to glory, I say, thank you. Sincerely.

P.S.

I declare with all humility that I am just a man. Books written by men are in many ways most imperfect in the light of that one great book written by the hand of our God, the Holy Bible. In my depictions of events in the lives of the disciples and peoples of Biblical days, I have taken liberty using Bible manners and customs to convey the drama of certain events. To those great saints who were actually there with Jesus, I extend my apology for any such dramatic liberties that most surely expose the limitations of current twenty-first century understanding of their life and times. When we meet at that great throne face-to-face, I will be most honored to hear your amazing stories from the glory of having been there.

~ Reader's Notes ~

I laughed, I cried ... and I shouted, "Yes!" all the way through. Great book! Thank you!" — J.J.W.

I never knew a real father until I read about my heavenly Father in this book. My natural father molested me when I was 13 years old, so you can understand that my idea of a father was very twisted. Thank you! I have found my real Father! — J.A.W.

For a long time my heart had been broken by events and people in my life. I felt there was no end to the grief... Every day became just like the other with no hope of every seeing any change. Then I had the opportunity to read this book, and everything changed. I found hope in the love of my Father toward those of a broken heart. There was new vision placed before me that filled my heart with joy and excitement. As you read these precious chapters you too will see the heart of the Father being poured out in so many ways to those who are in need of comfort, love, companionship and a "dad" who is there for you. It is a must read for today's uncertain world. — G.M.

This book gave me an incredible revelation of the fatherhood of God. It taught me not to fear God severely punishing me every time I made a mistake, but that I could come to Him and ask Him to forgive me... Thank-you for the incredible insight I gained from your book. Everyone must read this book as it will transform your life just as it did for me! — C.G.

Life With Our Father is the first book I have ever read that spoke about God's great desire to have a relationship with His children and then went on to explain what that looks like in our everyday lives. I appreciated how very practical and revealing this book was for me. I could easily see where I have given my heavenly Father much joy and much grief. All through the book I found myself saying, "Yes, that's great," and, "Oh no, I sure missed it there!" This is a life changing book. — S.S.

The Lord used this book to pull me out of one of the darkest periods in my life when all I could see was my own failures. I had slipped into a pit of despair, believing I was hopelessly lost. This book encouraged me that God is my Father, I am his child, He is not going to let me go, and He's not going to give up on me. — T.M.L.

This book melted my heart & changed my life. It helped me to see all my knowledge of the Word was not the same as experiential knowledge of my Father. It literally changed how I saw the Word of God as not just information on a page... Mercy became real to me. This book takes you to His heart, to where the Lord's heart is today: with His people - with you and me. — J.S.G.

TABLE OF CONTENTS

Introduction - Your Better Life is Waiting 1
Part One - The Father's Desire 3
    Chapter 1: Through His Eyes 5
    Chapter 2: The Tearing of the Veil 21
    Chapter 3: He Chose to be Called Father 33
Part Two - With Him In His School 39
    Chapter 4: Growing Up Begins at Birth 41
    Chapter 5: Gaining All by Knowing Him 49
    Chapter 6: The Teacher In Us 57
    Chapter 7: How We Learn 62
    Chapter 8: Divine Teaching Techniques 70
    Chapter 9: Learning that "We Can Do It" 75
    Chapter 10 Fatherly Discipline 85
    Chapter 11: The Parts of Chastisement 93
Part Three - Run-Aways 103
    Chapter 12: Unacceptable Fear 105
    Chapter 13: Free to Choose or Refuse 117
Part Four - With Him In His House 131
    Chapter 14: A Place for You 133
    Chapter 15: The Fullness of His House 144
    Chapter 16: In His Fellowship 159
    Chapter 17: In His Light 167
    Chapter 18: Eternal Opportunities 172
Part Five - With Him In His Fields 183
    Chapter 19: The Farmer's Children 185
    Chapter 20: Advancement by Faithfulness 189
    Chapter 21: With Him Where He Is 195
    Chapter 22: Thirty - Sixty - Hundredfold 201
    Chapter 23: Do What He Is Doing 206

Part Six - With Him In Fullness **215**
   Chapter 24: I Am My Father's Child.. 217
   Chapter 25: Manifesting His Glory... 226
   Chapter 26: Mature Thinking... 232

Part Seven - Conclusion **239**
   Chapter 27: We Owe it All to Him 241

INTRODUCTION

Your Better Life is Waiting

Look there in the garden where night blanketed a lone man bent in desperate prayer. Tears streamed to his hands stained by agony's blood. He knew his time had come, time to die for his friends, for us, for his Father.

And yet he did not weep in fear of death. Not this man. He wept rather of the impending brief separation that he knew was coming. He knew he must go, but the thought of being away from his friends was nearly more than his human frame could bear, and so he asked, "Father..., if there is another way..., please...," knowing full well that there was not.

And then the night was over. The day had come with his horrifying final task at hand. He knew what was coming; the humiliation, the executioner's hammer, the flesh-tearing pain, the slow death, and the bitter taste of countless sins not of his own doing. And he saw your face, my face, and the face of his Father.

Indeed our destiny hung in the balance, but it was his Father who he sought to please. And his Father's pleasure was you and I. Thousands of years had passed, dozens of generations, since the Father walked in the garden with his children. The Father wanted his babies back. And he was about to get them. Jesus was going to the Cross.

Are you weary of living your life in cycles of rights and wrongs? Are you tired of just surviving life's storms? *This is not God's plan for you! You can change that starting today.*

Do you feel distant from your heavenly Father and far from His heart? Would you really like to know the God who created you? *You can know Him more intimately than you have ever imagined!*

Are you ready for a better life that will not rust, decay or fade away? *That better life is waiting. Come and take it!*

Life With Our Father, is both a revelation of our God as *He* desires us to see Him, and a very practical guide to understanding His ways, His house, and growing up in His life. This book will open your eyes to His amazing plan and inspire you to take hold of the better life that He has already prepared for you.

Please join me in this life-changing journey into the passionate and gentle heart of our heavenly Father.

James E. Laero
Author

PART ONE

THE FATHER'S DESIRE

The greatest power in the universe works through the desire of the heavenly Father to be with you.

Chapter 1

Through His Eyes

Bill hovered over me waving a pair of razor sharp scissors as he talked, "I keep trying to be good. Everything goes OK for a while but then I just seem to slip right back into that stuff again. I'm so tired of trying. It never seems to change. I think God is disgusted with me." Bill paused and sighed, "I might as well just give up."

I was getting my monthly haircut when Bill, the hair stylist, made his declaration of defeat. Moments earlier, after telling him I wanted an inch or so off the top, he asked me where I lived and what I did for a living. I never met Bill before that moment, having just popped into the first hair salon I saw on my walk through the local mall. I told him I ministered at a church about thirty miles up the road. Bill went on to tell me his story as a member of a large church and about his frustration trying to find the life he saw in other Christians.

Bill had a big problem, and little of it had to do with his cycle of trying and failing to be good. His problem was not his ability, or lack of ability, to be good. Bill's problem was his vision. He couldn't see! No, he wasn't a blind stylist. But he sure was blind.

As Bill snipped away at my hair I spoke quietly to him about how much he was loved by his heavenly Father and what our part was in response to God's great gift of life through Jesus Christ. As I shook off the hair clippings I suggested a Bible scripture he might like to read. (As it turned out, another of his customers had given him a modern translation of the Bible just a week earlier.) Bill gave me his business card as I left and asked me to stop by again, even if I didn't need a haircut. I never saw Bill again. The salon closed shortly after my visit and Bill disappeared.

Driving home from that divinely arranged haircutting appointment I thought a lot about Bill's frustration and about the very real presence of God's desire to have Bill understand His love. When I spoke to Bill about the heart of God, the Holy Spirit's passion overflowed in me toward him. As strong as Bill's desire was to know God, his heavenly Father's desire to have Bill know Him was much more intense.

This divine desire of God for us to know Him is the foundation of everything our God has done since the fall in the garden, and it is still at the center of His heart to this day. Through thousands of years up to the time of the Cross, He worked and invested to make a way for us to be with Him. And then, as a magnificent climactic gesture of that love, He went as far as the sacrifice of His only Son so that He could regain all of us as sons and daughters. The Apostle Paul wrote of this master plan in his letter to the Ephesians:

How blessed is God! And what a blessing he is! He's the Father of our Master, Jesus Christ, and takes us to the high places of blessing in him. Long before he laid down earth's foundations, he had us in mind, had settled on us as the focus of his love, to be made whole and holy by his love. Long, long ago he decided to adopt us into his family through Jesus Christ. (What pleasure he took in planning this!)

Ephesians 1:3-5 (the Message)

Everyone has an image of God and what He is all about. This image comes to us from the teachings, experiences and observations we've been exposed to. Some people see God as a provider, others see Him as a protector, or as a distant mystical supreme being who created the earth and people as a weekend hobby project. And still there are others, like Bill, that see Him as a judge. If you surveyed a hundred people who confessed to be Christians, asking them who God is, what He is like and what He expects of them, you would likely end up with nearly as many different answers.

The way we view our heavenly Father is critical to every part of our life. The images we hold of Him will determine whether we gain or miss the great glory that is available to us now, in this life. God tells us in His Word that, *"According to our faith (in Him) it shall be done unto us."* To have faith in anyone we must know him or her. We must know their intent and their reliability. The same is true about our faith in our heavenly Father. If we are ever to gain anything from Him we must have faith in Him. To have faith in Him, true faith, we must get to know Him. *Be encouraged, reader! You are already on your way to knowing Him better.*

God was passionate for me to tell Bill that He loved him. And though I did tell him, a thick cloud of hopelessness still hung over him. My simple words of encouragement, though temporarily uplifting to his heart, were not enough. He was not languishing because God had abandoned him; but rather he was buried in a pit of desperation as a result of his own lack of vision. When we fail to see God properly, we end up living in needless cycles of fear and frustration.

My people are being destroyed because they don't know me.
Hosea 4:6a (NLT)

Too often we lose sight of, and more often totally fail to understand, as did Bill, that the greatest desire of this all-powerful God is to be a *Father* to us. Bill was stuck in defeat because of a faulty image of God as being only his executioner.

Indeed, when Bill looked at God he saw a judge. Then of course, when he looked honestly at his own life, he saw things that needed to be judged. The result for Bill was endless frustration in his daily cycle of measuring out all the good, bad, right, wrong, success and failure of his life in an attempt to feel justified. What an awful way to live. God doesn't want anyone to live such a life of frustration.

Bill's poor *vision* of God left him blind to the true full glorious work of Jesus Christ. Worse yet, no one ever led Bill to the God who is his Father. In his blinded condition, Bill couldn't see the gentleness and patience of his Father's heart. He didn't see that salvation as a spiritual growing-up process much like we grow up in our natural lives. He didn't know about the provision that his heavenly Father had put in the church to help him come to fullness and maturity, and he didn't see the true desire of God's heart, which is now, and always has been, to fellowship with us.

If we fail to understand what really motivates our heavenly Father, we are doomed to a life of frustration and failure. To gain the fullness He desires for us, and return to Him the desire of His own heart, we need only learn to see things through His eyes, to get His perspective.

Your perspective of life can mean the difference between absolute peace and absolute terror. Let me ask you a question. Have you ever been so gripped by fear that it tore through your very soul? I mean the kind of fear that sweeps through you head-to-toe in dreadful waves wondering what might come next. Some two thousand years ago such fear seized the hearts of some very strong men crossing the Sea of Galilee. They survived their fateful journey. Along the way their encounter with the Son of God became forever etched into eternity's record of Christ's amazing miracles. But more important than the miracle they witnessed was the lesson they learned about their Father's perspective. Their journey is recorded in the Gospel of Mark, Chapter 4. Let's ride along with them for a distance.

***

"JOHN!! JAMES!! COME OVER HERE!!" shouted Peter.

"What's up?" questioned John, brushing by him on his way to the beach.

Peter replied, "Jesus wants the boats. We are crossing over."

"Now? It is nearly dark!" exclaimed John.

"Yes John. Now," commanded Peter.

John paused to think and answered, "OK. I'll get them ready, but hey Peter?"

Peter halted in the sand, "Yes John?"

"Do you think I can ride with the Master?" asked John with a grin.

"Yes John. Now go get the boats!" Peter replied watching as his young friend bounced away to the older disciples now gathering belongings for the journey.

"Hey James! Did you hear? I get to ride in the Master's boat!" boasted John.

"Who said?" demanded James. "I asked Peter and he said I could." retorted John proudly.

"Wait here," responded James.

"Where are you going?" John shouted off to James already jogging up the beach.

"I'm going to talk to Peter. I want to ride with Jesus too," James shouted over his shoulder back to John.

"PETER!! HEY PETER!!!" called James, now half out of breath.

Life With Our Father

Peter, who was caring for the pre-launch work needed for the lead boat, responded without looking up, "Yes James. What is it?"

"John said that you told him he could ride in the Master's boat," James spoke more quietly as he noticed Peter intent on his work.

"Yes James. I did," Peter responded knowing what was coming next.

"Can I be in His boat too?" asked James. "Yes, I suppose so," Peter responded without turning his gaze from the work at hand.

"Great!" James half shouted. "Hey did you see all those people listening to the Master teach today? How many do you think were there?" he asked.

Peter half sighed, weary from the long day, "I don't know, James, a lot."

"Peter?" James continued, "Those stories he told, about the farmer and the mustard seed, did you understand it all?" James asked quietly.

Peter paused from his work for the first time in their conversation and, looking out over the sea before them, replied, "No, James, not all of it. But I'm sure He will tell us what it means. Can you help your brother John get the boats ready?"

"Yes. I'm going now. Who are you riding with Peter?" asked an excited James.

"I don't know yet. Maybe with you guys," smiled Peter.

James raced away up the beach as Peter paused again just briefly to enjoy the zeal of his brother trotting away.

Just then, the Master, still pressed by the crowd, arrived at the shoreline. Peter was amazed. "How could a man go so long without rest?" he whispered to himself. Turning up the shoreline he cried, *"EVERYONE IN THE BOATS! IT'S TIME*

TO GO!" Counting heads quickly he questioned, "Where are Andrew and Phillip?"

"We are here. What is it?" Philip asked just walking in from the other edge of the crowd with Andrew.

"Get Bartholomew and Thomas. Tell them to get into the boats. We are crossing over the lake," Peter said as he threw their last few belongings onto the second boat.

"Now Peter? It will be dark before we get across!" said a concerned Andrew.

"Yes. Now," Peter replied hurriedly as he drew up his tunic and moved back up the shoreline towards the Master's boat.

"OK. Whatever you say," agreed Andrew, *"HEY!! EVERYONE INTO THE BOATS!! WE ARE LEAVING!!"* he shouted waving his hands over his head, *"PUSH OFF!! WE'RE CROSSING NOW!"*

***

With all the boats on their way John was the first to speak, "What a day! Did you see the size of those crowds? It was amazing! How many do you think there were Peter?"

"More than I could count, they just kept coming," Peter replied breaking off a piece of bread. Leaning to the rail of the boat, he continued, "Did you see how they hung on every word the Master spoke? They were still calling out to Him right up to the time He got into the boat. We should have stayed another day. I bet they would have all come back tomorrow! What do you think James?"

"I don't know," James rubbed his chin as he responded, "But I can't wait to see what happens next. The Master is becoming famous. Everyone wants to see Him. I think He could go far."

"Yes, I think He could become king of all Israel! I think we could march right into Jerusalem tomorrow and take over," Peter's voice rose with excitement as he spoke.

"YES! That's what I was thinking! Has He said anything yet? Do you think He will do it?" asked James as he pulled a piece of bread for himself and John."

"No James. He hasn't said anything about it to me," replied Peter, "But He must know how many people want to make Him King."

John froze in place for a moment staring out into the dark night in front of the boat. "Hey Peter, did you feel that?" he asked quietly."

"Feel what John?" Peter asked still thinking about a possible triumphant day to come in Jerusalem.

"That breeze," replied John with concern, "There it is again. Did you feel it?" he asked.

Peter set his bread aside and stood to his feet, "Yes. I felt it," he replied pulling his mantle up closer to his neck.

"Do you think a storm is coming?" questioned John.

"I don't know. It's hard to tell on this lake. The storms come so quickly here," Peter paused for a moment to listen to the growing winds. He turned to look off beyond the stern of the boat through the murky darkness to the boats that followed. "Better tell the others to be careful," he half whispered to himself." Just then a gust of wind swept across the deck. Peter spun around and exclaimed, "James, call out to the other boats and tell them to watch out for........," caught in mid-sentence Peter grabbed for the rudder as the next gust of wind rocked the boat, "TOO LATE!! HERE IT COMES!" shouted Peter.

The disciples scrambled for anything to hold to. "It's a bad one Peter! I saw one like this a few years ago," someone shouted from Peter's left, the noise of the storm now too great to know who, "Six fishermen were drowned when they tried to...," the voice trailed off in the din of the wind and waves.

The storm raged on, growing with a fury by the minute. "What do we do?" cried John to Peter the fisherman.

"John! Take the rudder!" commanded Peter, "James! Grab the oars! *AND EVERYONE HOLD ON!!*" screamed Peter now fearing the worst himself. He had never seen one like this.

"*Peter!! The waves!! They're coming over the sides!! We will be swamped!!*" exclaimed John.

"*Hold it into the wind John!*" Peter cried back as loudly as he could but the sound of his words seemed only to be sucked away into the menacing gray waves now filling the boat.

"*Peter!! Peter!! We're breaking up!*" cried James.

"*Row, James, row!*" Peter shouted and motioned with his arms.

"*We'll never make it!! The boat is nearly full!*" came a voice that Peter thought was John's.

"*Row!*" Peter yelled, his mind now tinged with a growing fear that he had never known on any voyage through his years on the sea.

"*Hang on!! Here comes a big one!* Someone screamed from the stern as voices now mixed beyond recognition in the melee. *Grab the buckets!!! We need to bail out the water!!*" "*What?*" "*The buckets!!*" "*I can't hear you!!*" "*The buckets!! Bail out the water!!*" "*But the rudder...*" "*Forget the rudder!! It's useless in this!! Bail!! Bail!!*"

"*Peter!! It's not working. We can't bail fast enough!! We're going down. We're going to drown!! What do we do?*" "*Jesus!! Master!! Where is He?*"

"*He's still asleep!*" "*What! I can't believe it! Doesn't He know what is happening? What is wrong with Him??? We are all going to die!! Doesn't He care about us?*" "*Jesus!! Master!! We are going to drown!! Don't you care?*"

Quietly the Master arose to the deck of the boat. "Hush. Be still," He said to the winds. And just as suddenly as they came, they were gone. And then turning to His friends he asked, "Peter, James, John, why were you so easily alarmed? Do you still have no confidence in me?" Jesus quietly turned to his resting place as the disciples gathered the boat's equipment and supplies.

"Peter. The storm. It is gone! Vanished! This is unbelievable. He stopped a storm with only a few words. Who is this man?" whispered John.

"I saw it," replied Peter softly, "Did you see His eyes?"

"His eyes?" John asked as he slid up next to Peter on the deck. What about His eyes?"

"When he spoke to us…..his eyes…..they looked right through me when he asked us why we had awakened him," Peter said as he watched the Master slip back to his pillow, "What else could we have done? We were about to die," he said with quietness in his voice.

"Yes," Andrew spoke up from across the deck, "I felt it too. It seemed the storm meant nothing to him," Andrew said with amazement, "What does all this mean?"

"I don't know, John," Peter responded quietly, "I don't know."

***

Two Perspectives - Ours and His

How many times have you found yourself in just such circumstances? I know I have. Pressed by the storms of life, crushed under what seem to be fatal waves of tribulation, scared to death, racked by fear. Imagine yourself in that boat during that terrifying storm. What would you have done? It seems only reasonable to cry for help in such a situation. So why did Jesus rebuke the disciples for their lack of faith? Why was He disappointed? Doesn't God want us to cry out for help in times of trouble? The disciples were frightened. They simply called to Him for help. And anyhow, it was Jesus who set them onto the lake that evening. This was His fault. So why did they get rebuked?

To the disciples the storm meant sure death. They were convinced of impending doom. They did what was natural in that situation. They acted on their own understanding. They were simply evaluating the situation through their natural senses, seeing it through their own eyes, from their own perspective. But *that* was the problem - their perspective.

Jesus was on the same boat as the disciples. He was in the same storm. But unlike the disciples, He was resting comfortably. How could Jesus sleep through such danger? The answer is - perspective. To Him the storm held no danger because He knew that there was not a storm big enough to keep Him from fulfilling His Father's will. Jesus knew that He was not destined to perish in a storm. He knew that the Father had sent Him to give His life up on a cross. Jesus knew the Father perfectly and was resting in His Father's perspective.

The disciples relied on their own perspective of the storm and fell into fear followed by terror. We fear when we fail to see the events of life God's way. We fail to see it His way for one simple reason - we don't yet know Him. But there is great hope for us. He has made a way for us to know Him, and in that, a way to a much better life.

As humans, we tend to look through our own eyes at the workings and motives of God. This is a youthful, man-centered viewpoint. Proverbs 3:5 instructs us to

"Trust in the LORD with all thine heart; and lean not unto thine own understanding." (KJV)

If we want to know God, to understand Him and His ways in our life, we must see though His eyes. We must have His understanding. Jesus was able to sleep through the storm because He understood the Father's love for not only the men in that boat, but for all creation - past, present and future. He was not going to die in that storm and He knew it. He knew that it was not His time. He had His Dad's perspective. And so, He just rested. Wow. Don't you wish you could live that way through the storms of your life? You can!

What does God want?

So why did these men receive a rebuke after such a terrifying ordeal? What did God expect from them?

The real issue, which they did not yet understand, was relationship. In their terror the disciples opened their mouths and accused Jesus of not caring. Look carefully again at what they asked Him:

> *Jesus was sleeping at the back of the boat with his head on a cushion. The disciples woke him up, shouting, "Teacher, <u>don't you care</u> that we're going to drown?"*
> Mark 4:38 (NLT)

The accusation by the disciples that Jesus didn't care if they drowned was quite an insult. His very presence on the earth was to lay down His life for them one day very soon on a rough wooden cross. Here He was, the Son of God come to die in humiliation, so that they could be with the heavenly Father forever, and they were accusing Him of not caring. Look at how Jesus responded to their accusation:

> *Getting to his feet, he told the wind, "Silence!" and the waves, "Quiet down!" They did it. The lake became smooth as glass. Then he said to his disciples, "Why can't you trust me?"*

Luke 8:24-25 (The Message)

The disciples had walked with Him and witnessed His love to others; His healings, His preaching, His tender care. And yet they could not believe that they were safe riding in the same boat with Him. They couldn't believe that He loved them enough and was a good enough friend to keep them safe through that storm. And they went right ahead and said that to Him. They accused Him of not caring. It was this accusation that brought the gentle rebuke from Jesus. God never rebukes us for calling for help. But He is insulted when we accuse Him of not caring, and is offended when we don't have faith in His love.

The gentle questioning rebuke, which Jesus spoke after calming the storm, had little to do with how great their faith was in His ability to control weather patterns; the issue there in that storm centered on relationship! He did not care much about their confidence in His almighty powers. He didn't come to earth to wow us. He came to be the way home to the Father. The tone of disappointment in His question came as a result of their lack of confidence in His love for them. He counted them as His friends and they doubted Him. They had traveled with Him and personally witnessed His love to all mankind and yet they doubted His personal care of them.

Anyone can believe in the power of God. History and the Bible both record cases of godly and ungodly men and women who believed in and acknowledged the power of God. Cain, the son of Adam who murdered his brother; Pharaoh, the prince of Egypt who tortured God's people; those who perished in Noah's day, and even Satan himself, all acknowledged the power of God. God cares little about who believes or does not believe in His power. If that was all He wanted, He could simply pour out His miraculous supernatural power over the earth in a thousand different ways every day.

What God wants is relationship with His children. It was this desire for relationship (fellowship) with His friends that prompted Jesus to ask His disciples why they had no confidence in Him on that boat. He was disappointed because in spite of all of the compassion and love they had witnessed while traveling with Him, they still doubted His love for them.

Indeed, Jesus had not come to set up an earthly kingdom or to just display the Father's supernatural power on the earth. In His own words, He came *"to do the will of the Father."* The will of the Father had not changed from the beginning since the time of the first people, Adam and Eve, in the garden. The will of the Father is to be with His children, to be with you and me.

The disciples on the boat did not yet see Jesus as the way to the Father. They had no perception whatsoever of the Father's ultimate desire of fellowship with them. If they had understood this divine desire they would have never feared the dangers of a simple storm. In their youthful ignorance they saw Jesus only in what He needed to do for them now - deliverance from a bad storm. They were like little children who cry when a parent fails to respond to a perceived danger as quickly as the child wishes. This is acceptable when children are small and have not yet learned to trust the love of their parents. But these men had been with Jesus and had witnessed His love and care first hand. In spite of this, they still had not come to understand the one issue that guaranteed their safety in that storm. They failed to see the heart-motive behind the power that would quiet that storm, which was their heavenly Father's love for them. In years to follow these same men would grow in the knowledge of their God to the point they would not even fear death by torture. One day they would come to know personally what motivated the heart of their God. In time they would become pillars of the church and examples of how to walk in glorious relationship with the Father.

The greatest power in the universe works through the desire of our heavenly Father to be with you and me. In the disciples' failure to understand and have faith in this, "relationship based power," they offended the Lord and the Father, and plunged their own hearts into unnecessary fear. The disciples would have reached shore just as safely if they had believed in Jesus' love and simply rested with Him through the storm. Easier said than done? Yes maybe - but not impossible. If you will believe, all things are possible to you through Him. If you know the Father, you can rest through life's storms and you will reach the other shore safely because He will always respond to such confident *relationship-based* faith.

A proper and practical understanding of our Father's desire is foundational to every area of our life, from surviving the everyday storms of life to understanding life in the school of His Holy Spirit. We become more than victorious when we understand His motives. Lacking His perspective and failing to understand His heart condemns us to suffer in endless cycles of fear and frustration, and we miss the opportunity to rest in and enjoy His fellowship. This lack of understanding also robs Him of His ultimate desire, which is to be with us. Bill, the hair stylist, was caught in exactly this cycle of frustration, never really seeing how his heavenly Father really viewed him.

There is no need for you to tremble at the storms of life. There is no reason for you to fear failure, or loss, or even death. There is no reason to give up. He loves you dearly. He understands you completely. From before the foundation of the earth He knew you. He knows all of your weaknesses, all of your pains, all of your fears and all of your needs. You need never cry out questioning His care for you. He cares more than you can imagine. He has a plan for you - a good plan.

It won't be long before this generous God who has great plans for us in Christ — eternal and glorious plans they are! — will have you put together and on your feet for good.
1 Peter 5:10 (The Message)

His greatest desire is to live with His children, to be with *you.* All of history is His love story showing how He moved and worked to bring us all to His house. We need never doubt our place in His hands! In Him we are more than just storm survivors, we are eternal children of the Most High God, born to rule, reign and live with Him. If you are willing to learn of His ways, you can fellowship with Him now in a great richness and enjoy the better life He destined for you.

So how do we get to know the Father? He is not visible. He is not physically here. But thanks be to God! He sent His Son Jesus Christ and made Himself known by Him.

he that hath seen me hath seen the Father (Jesus speaking)
John 14:9b (KJV)

Now we can look through His eyes. Now you and I can know the Father. We can see Him today!

Chapter 2

The Tearing of the Veil

What was God the Father doing while Jesus was on the Cross? How did He view the crucifixion? When I was a young Christian I believed that during the crucifixion the heavenly Father was sitting up above on a big white throne wringing His hands in silent agony until it was all over. My perspective has completely changed. I believe the Father's focus was on a building a few blocks away from the hill where Jesus died and He was excited at what was about to happen. And when His Son finished His mission on that Cross, you may be surprised what He did next.

But before we see it through His eyes, let's take a look at the crucifixion the way the disciples may have seen it.

***

Then Jesus shouted out again, and he gave up his spirit. At that moment the curtain in the Temple was torn in two, from top to bottom. The earth shook, rocks split apart, and tombs opened. The bodies of many godly men and women who had died were raised from the dead after Jesus' resurrection. They left the cemetery, went into the holy city of Jerusalem, and appeared to many people.
Matthew 27:50-53 (NLT)

"Peter. Peter is that you?" called John

"Yes John," came a quiet voice from the bushes of the courtyard.

"Peter. Why are you hiding there in the shadows? Peter, you've been crying. What it is? Do you weep for the Master?" asked John.

"No John," replied Peter.

"Then what Peter? John asked, "I have never seen you weep like this before."

"I did a terrible thing today, John," Peter replied dropping his face into his hands.

"What Peter? What did you do?" John asked.

Peter brushed the dampness from his cheeks and between sobs said, "I followed the crowd that took the Master away today. They were treating Him like a common thief John, shouting curses and humiliating Him. They took Him to the high priest. I followed them into the courtyard and stood by the fire with the temple guards, and John, do you know what they did to him?" John sat silently as Peter continued, "I heard them screaming at Him inside. They were holding court. They were accusing Him of all kinds of wickedness and treason."

"But why, Peter? What did He do?" asked John.

"He did nothing," replied Peter quietly.

"Then why did they take him away? What does this all mean, Peter?" John asked.

"I don't know, John. I don't know," Peter said as he stood to look back towards the temple.

"But what did you do? Why were you weeping?" John asked again as he stood next to Peter and placed his hand on his shoulder.

Tears returned to Peters eyes as he went on, "After the shouting stopped… they…" Peter fell to his knees, as he could speak no more.

"Peter, what is it? What happened after the shouting stopped?" John asked desperately.

A full minute passed until Peter could regain his composure, he responded, "They were beating Him, John. I heard them punching Him and slapping Him! I couldn't bear to listen. John, they beat the Master!"

"They beat Him! Why? What is happening, Peter? Why is this happening?" John said as he too now wept at the thought of his friend Jesus being beaten.

"I don't know, John. I don't know," replied Peter.

The first light of morning began to creep over the hills as Peter and John sat there quietly together. They had not spoken for a long while when John heard Peter begin to softly weep, "Peter, you are crying again. What is it?' asked John.

"John, do you remember what the Master told me at supper when I said that I would never leave Him?" Peter asked quietly, humbly.

"Yes, Peter, I remember. He said you would deny Him three times," John responded softly.

"It happened, John. It happened just the way He said it would. While I was standing with the guards in the courtyard, a girl came up to me and asked if I was one of the Master's disciples. John, I said No! I said No, John! Three times! I betrayed Him three times! They were all staring at me and I... I..." Peter's voice crumbled away in his sobs again.

John waited a moment and then, placing his hand on his friend's shoulder, asked, "What Peter? What did you say?"

"I told them that I did not know Him!' Peter screamed through his weeping, "I betrayed Him like a coward, John. Oh, John... they were beating Him... and I... I denied Him! I acted as though I never knew Him! Oh God help me! Help me! *MY MASTER! HELP ME! WHAT HAVE I DONE??* John! What have I done?? What should I do??" Peter fell face down to the earth.

"I don't know, Peter," John responded kneeling beside his elder friend, "I am no better than you. I also ran when they took Him away,"

Peter pulled himself slowly to his feet. They walked together quietly a ways and as they were about to part John asked, "Did you hear what they are going to do with Him now?"

Peter turned to John and said, "I overheard one of the guards saying that they were to bring Him to Pilate tomorrow."

John was visibly shaken by Peter's response and said, "*PILATE* - but why? What are they thinking? Why would they bring Him to Pilate? Pilate is a Roman! We are Jews. What does this mean Peter?"

"John, we are not safe. They are searching for the Master's disciples. We need to get off the streets and into hiding until all this blows over," Peter warned, "Do you understand John?"

"Yes Peter," John responded, "But what will they do to Jesus?" He asked.

Peter had enough of the day. He was spent and in need of a safe place to just close his eyes to it all. "I don't know, John. Maybe tomorrow..., I just don't know," Peter mumbled back as he turned to go.

John watched quietly as his friend walked off into the morning sun and then moved off quickly to find anyone who might have news of his Master.

***

John raced along the shoreline desperately searching the docks and boats for Peter. He found him in the stern of a boat tending a net alone. *"PETER! PETER!"* exclaimed John.

"John! What is it?" Peter asked dropping his net. He could see the fear in his young friend's face as he approached.

"Peter! Did you hear?" John asked as he rushed to Peter's side.

"What, John, What?" Peter asked as he reached out with both hands to brace up John's shoulders in front of him. John was exhausted and soaked with perspiration.

"Peter! *THEY ARE GOING TO KILL HIM!*" blurted John, "I just heard it! They are taking Him to be crucified! Peter! They are taking Him to His death! What should we do? *THEY ARE GOING TO KILL THE MASTER!*"

Peter felt his knees weaken at John's report. The blood drained from his face. His mind raced. *"BUT WHY, JOHN? WHAT DID THEY SAY HE DID?"* he asked.

"I don't know! They were all screaming and calling for His death!" John said as he began to weep softly. "Peter! What can we do? Why is Jehovah letting this happen?" he asked.

Peter had no words to answer. Turning he walked slowly back to his nets.

"I'm going!" John cried.

"Where are you going, John?" asked Peter. "I'm going to the hill where they are taking Him to be executed." John turned and ran back up the shoreline without another word. Peter returned to his work with a rekindled memory of his betrayal pressing heavy on his heart. Again the tears began to fall as he plunged his face into the coarse fibers of the net he had been mending.

***

Peter's heart jumped as he heard footsteps racing to his front door. *"PETER! PETER! PETER ARE YOU HOME?"* John cried while banging at Peter's door.

"Yes, John. Come in," replied Peter, "What is it?"

John was breathless as he asked, "Did you see the storm? Did you feel the earth shake?"

"Yes." Peter answered, "It nearly brought down my roof."

"IT WAS HIM PETER!" John exclaimed, "He was hanging there on the cross, they were laughing at Him and cursing Him and then He cried out and said, It is finished! And He died! I began to weep but then the ground under my feet shook and the rocks split open right before my eyes! And did you hear what happened in the temple?"

John was talking so fast that Peter could barely keep up. "The temple? The temple is on the other side of town! What happened in the temple, John?" Peter asked.

Grabbing for Peter's arm, John nearly screamed, *"THE VEIL!* They said the veil in the temple ripped in two from top to bottom!"

"WHAT? IMPOSSIBLE!" pronounced Peter incredulously, "How could the veil tear? I know for a fact that the veil is as thick as my forearm at least!"

"I KNOW! BUT IT TORE IN HALF!" John insisted, "What do you think it means, Peter?"

"I don't know," Peter responded, "I don't know what it could mean, but truly, He was the Son of God."

***

The Father's View of the Crucifixion

Just imagine the confusion and trauma of the disciples as their Master Jesus went to His death. The Scriptures tell us that they scattered like lost sheep. Even after walking with Him for three years during His earthly ministry they still had not yet come to comprehend the real meaning of His presence on the earth. And when the veil of the temple tore, they had no idea of the significance of the event. But it was a defining moment for the heavenly Father.

These moments surrounding the death of the Son of God have been dramatized in books, plays, and movies, countless times through many generations. To this day, however, I have yet to see a depiction of the fullness of those last moments as they have been recorded here in God's word. In each case the writers, directors and producers skip over one of the most dramatic and exciting parts of the last few moments of Jesus' time on the Cross. They fail to depict the heavenly Father's view of the crucifixion. In failing to do so, the full revelation of the crucifixion is missed badly. This missing perspective is critical to you and me. To even begin to comprehend the depth of God's love for us (which was worked through the Cross) we must know how He himself viewed His Son's horrible death. We need to see what the crucifixion meant to Him, the Father, personally.

All church-attending Christians hear sermons and teachings about what the crucifixion means to us; forgiveness of sins, deliverance from evil, eternal life, peace, joy, provision, acceptance into His house, etc. These are all critical doctrines to our new faith in God, but these are man centered and only the first and most basic of truths. The Apostle Paul called them, spiritual milk. To get the meat of the message of the Cross we must begin to think higher. We must consider what this moment in time meant to our heavenly Father. When we see the crucifixion through His eyes, we get a new revelation, not only of how much He was willing to sacrifice to save you and I from damnation, but also a clear and dramatic insight into how passionate He was, and is, about having us with Him as His children, as His friends.

To unfold this revelation from the biblical account of the crucifixion, first consider the magnitude of what was happening on that hillside that fateful day. Jesus, the heavenly Father's only Son, was hanging on a rough wooden rack with nails driven violently through His hands and feet, bleeding from a wound in His side, agonizing through this slow humiliating form of public execution, which was generally reserved only for the worst of criminals. And Jesus was innocent. He was not only innocent of any crime against the local and national governments, but He was without any sin in His entire life. He had never offended His heavenly Father. This was God's only perfect son, dying alone without the Father intervening. Where was the Father? To understand the answer to that question we must first travel back in time to a meeting God had with a man on top of a mountain.

Long before the day of Jesus' crucifixion, God met with a man named Moses for forty days and forty nights on a mountain called Sinai. Moses and God's people had just been miraculously delivered out of hundreds of years of slavery to Pharaoh in Egypt. They were on their way from Egypt to the Promised Land. When they reached Mount Sinai, God called Moses for a meeting. During that meeting God gave Moses commandments for the children of Israel to live by, and instructed Moses in the building of a tabernacle (or house), where God Himself would live with them as they traveled through the wilderness on their way to the Promised Land.

Seven full chapters in the book of Exodus cover the design, construction and use of the Tabernacle. In Exodus chapter 29 verses 43 through 46, God reveals the purpose of that tabernacle:

> *I will meet the people of Israel there, in the place made holy by my glorious presence. Yes, I will consecrate the Tabernacle and the altar, and I will consecrate Aaron and his sons to serve me as priests. Then I will live among the people of Israel and be their God, and they will know that I am the Lord their God. I am the one who brought them out of the land of Egypt so that I could live among them. I am the Lord their God.* (NLT)

There is that divine plan of the Father again - to be with us, and for us to be with Him. But inside that Tabernacle there was a problem. It was called, the veil.

The original Tabernacle (later to be the fixed Temple in Jerusalem) was a tent structure designed with the ability to be taken down and set up as the Israelites traveled through the wilderness and into the Promised Land. It was made up of an outer surrounding court and an inner court with two rooms, the Holy Place and the Most Holy Place. The Most Holy Place (the place where God would dwell) was separated from the other room by a thick cloth curtain (or veil):

> *"Set up this Tabernacle according to the pattern you were shown on the mountain. "For the inside of the Tabernacle, make a special curtain of finely woven linen. Hang the inner curtain from clasps, and put the Ark of the Covenant in the room behind it. This curtain will <u>separate</u> the Holy Place from the Most Holy Place."*
> Exodus 26:30-31a, 33 (NLT)

God's problem with the veil is that it *separated* Him from us. God did not want to be separated from us. But that is exactly what that veil did. In that old tabernacle, behind the veil in that small room known as, The Holy of Holies, God would meet with Moses and the high priests alone, and then only a few men out of each generation for hundreds of years. By the time Jesus arrived at the Cross, the Tabernacle had become a large elaborate temple that rested inside the city of Jerusalem - only a short distance from Mount Calvary where Jesus was crucified.

To understand our heavenly Father's view of the crucifixion we must fully appreciate how much He despised the old imperfect tabernacle/temple system of living with His people. With every part of His being He wanted to be with His people in fullness. It had been many generations since He had walked with His creation in the garden. Since the original sin of His first man, and the separation it caused, he longed to regain His place in the lives of His people.

The old temple system, and the room behind the veil, must have been like a cage to the heart of our Father. Not in the sense that He was in any way bound to its bars involuntarily, but in the sense that it was the only way sinful men could even get close to Him until the crucifixion of His Son on the Cross. Why? It is because God is light and in Him is no darkness. If you turn on a light in a dark room the darkness is simply destroyed. If you have darkness in your heart and you step into the presence of God's perfect light what do you think would happen? That is why God could not see His children face-to-face until Jesus paid for our sins wiping out our darkness. That is why there was a veil in that tabernacle. Imagine having children but you cannot be with them except on the other side of a big curtain. That is what our Father faced because of our sins.

God wanted an end to this imperfect dwelling place. He worked through many generations in preparation for that moment in which His only Son would die as the last and perfect payment for your and my sins. Because Jesus was perfect, without sin, the sacrifice of His life would be all that was needed to once and for all pay the debt for sin and eliminate the need for a veil between the Father and His children.

As Jesus suffered those last few hours, the Father waited in glorious anticipation for that moment when that old stone-and-earth-built Tabernacle, and its restrictive veil of separation, would no longer be needed. At the moment of Jesus's death, I believe the Father had both of His great big holy hands on that thick veil of separation. And at the very second when Jesus gave his last gasp and died, I believe the Father violently and triumphantly ripped that now worthless veil of separation right down the middle from top to bottom. And then, full of joy, He danced! Or at least I personally believe He did. I believe He danced with such zeal that He shook the earth all around Jerusalem, splitting rocks and cracking open tombs.

Glory! Glory! It was finally finished! He could finally live in the hearts of anyone who accepted the sacrifice of His Son in faith! You! Me! Anyone! He wants to be with *EVERYONE*. He desires that not even one be lost! No more curtains of separation! No more blood sacrifices! No more waiting to talk and walk with His beloved children! His plan through the ages was finished! No, He was not wringing His hands in agony! He knew His Son would rise again. He was standing at the hated veil of separation in confident anticipation of the moment that He had waited upon for generations - *to be with you and me.*

The old veil of the tabernacle, that curtain which had stood between the Father and His children, was no more. Jesus, by His death, eliminated the veil and became Himself the new passage to the Father. From that point on to this day, anyone who would believe on Jesus and His sacrifice could walk right into the very presence of the Father without any fear of condemnation or judgment.

What an amazing picture of how great His desire is to be with us. He couldn't wait even a few minutes after His only Son died. Full of desire for us, He literally shredded that veil of separation at the very moment His Son breathed His last breath on the Cross. Here is the passion of His desire: to be with His people completely, forever.

This is the force that compels our heavenly Father to this day. He continuously reaches out to us, desiring that we not miss this great gift of fellowship made possible by the sacrifice of His Son more than two thousand years ago. If, after everything He did for us on that day, we fail to grasp its true meaning, then the loss to Him and to us is truly tragic.

Through the death and resurrection of Jesus, our elder brother, we now have free access into the very presence of our Father. Because of Jesus we can be with our heavenly Father now, this very moment, without fear of rejection or condemnation. And by Jesus, the Father has his own desire, a dwelling place, with and in His Children.

And so, dear brothers and sisters, we can boldly enter heaven's Most Holy Place because of the blood of Jesus. By his death, Jesus opened a new and life-giving way through the curtain into the Most Holy Place. And since we have a great High Priest who rules over God's house, let us go right into the presence of God with sincere hearts fully trusting him. For our guilty consciences have been sprinkled with Christ's blood to make us clean, and our bodies have been washed with pure water.
Hebrews 10:19-22 (NLT)

Chapter 3

He Chose to be Called Father

"Daddy, up!" my first-born exclaimed as he reached his little arms out to me. Wow! My heart just melted. It was the first time I heard him say Daddy. As you can imagine, he got his wish. I scooped him right up and gave him a big hug. His simple words had filled my heart. That feeling of being called Daddy for the first time is one I will always cherish.

Look at this great revelation about our God's heart and plan:

> *And it came to pass, that, as he (Jesus) was praying in a certain place, when he ceased, one of his disciples said unto him, Lord, teach us to pray, as John also taught his disciples. And he said unto them, When ye pray, say, <u>Our Father</u> which art in heaven...*
> Luke 11:1-2a (KJV)

Throughout history God used many titles to describe Himself. Each name or title revealed a particular aspect of His person: Almighty God, Judge, Lord of Hosts, Most High God, King of Kings. But to you and me, His children, He chose the title of, "Father."

What we refer to as, the Lord's Prayer, here in the Gospel of Luke is an instructional outline that Jesus used when teaching His disciples how to pray. He started this simple prayer by teaching them the name to use when talking with God in prayer. Notice He did not teach them to address Him as, "Our King," or, "Our Judge," but as, "Our Father." Even though He is our king and He is a judge to all, He is *Father* to His children. As His children we have the special privilege of addressing Him as, Father. In this privilege is a powerful revelation of God's desires.

At the moment of salvation, that new birth in Him, He gives us His very own Spirit. When God's Spirit enters us, He compels us to call out to the Father just as a newborn cries out to its mother and father. The Holy Spirit immediately starts His work as a teacher by teaching us His name - the name of *Father*. More specifically, when the Spirit enters, He causes us to cry, "Abba, Father."

> *But when the time had fully come, God sent His Son, born of a woman, born under law, to redeem those under law, that we might receive the full rights of sons. Because you are sons, God sent the Spirit of His Son into our hearts, the Spirit who calls out, "<u>Abba</u>, Father."*
> Galatians 4:4-6 (NIV)

The word, Abba, is close to the English word, daddy. This word is more of a sound than an actual word. It is as a newborn that can't yet frame the whole word and sputters out, "da-da." Abba is baby language for, Father. In this personal title we begin to see how the title, Father, means much more than the positional head of a family.

When God calls Himself, Father, He is of course the head of His entire family. But to each individual child He is as close as, daddy. In my role as a parent I hold the title of father. To my children and their spouses however, I am not only, father, but also, dad. I am the head of our house, but to my children I am also the dad. I can be referred to as a father by anyone who knows I have children but the title, daddy, is one only my children can use. It comes to children as a birthright, by marriage or adoption.

The initial Spirit-born stirring in us to cry, Abba, or, daddy, is the foreshadowing of the ultimate purposes of our heavenly Father's desires. That cry of infancy is representative not only of our new position gained by adoption into His family, but also of His commitment and love to those who believe on Him. It tells us from the start that although He is Lord, King, and Master to all of creation; He is Father and, Daddy, to us.

This simple principle is a cornerstone to our understanding of God. It is the first of our great lessons and our first great comfort as new spiritual children. Every newborn Christian should know that he or she has a daddy in the fullest sense. Without the foundational understanding of the personal significance of, Abba, a child of God is left alone in the confusion and challenges of new life lacking the confidence of knowing He is there for them as any good father would be for his children. When it is neglected, we are robbed of the graces and joys of early childhood in the home of our new Dad.

When we gain the understanding that He is a Father to us, we can grow and learn in peace without fear of failure or rejection. When we learn to see Him as He wishes to be seen, as a good father, we become truly free to enjoy every part of His life. And we become a blessing to Him as we walk in the faith and trust that any child shows a good parent. It is His position to be honored and feared as a judge, king, and lord of lords, but it is His great joy and delight to be viewed as a father and daddy by His children.

How frustrating it must be to the Father to have invested so much through so many generations only to see us wrestle needlessly because of a failure to understand His heart and His plan as our Father.

Many Christians see God as an outside force judging their efforts as failures or successes from behind a cold throne while leaving them to work out their own perfection. They know that Jesus saves, but often never come to realize that Jesus saves us SO THAT we can be with the Father as His children.

In the book of Hosea, God declares that His people are destroyed because of lack of knowledge, or a lack of knowing what He is all about. When we fail to understand the true desire of God's heart, we end up in an endless cycle of frustration and confusion. In this state of ignorance we work and toil to be good, while wrestling with our troubled consciences after each failure. It was never meant to be this way. A good father would never expect his children to grow themselves up. Instead he would continue to invest his own life into theirs, nurturing them each step of the way, and never forsaking them when they stumble. This is the essence of a father. This is the character of our heavenly Father. Look at this great Scripture recorded in Philippians 2:13:

> *For God is working in you, giving you the desire and the power to do what pleases him.* (NLT)

Our Father not only desires us to be perfect, but He also works with us to make us *want* to be like Him, and, teaches us the ways to accomplish this lofty call. In fact, He enjoys the teaching process as much as the end results.

I vividly recall the first time my eldest son helped me with a household project. He was two years old at the time. Our vacuum cleaner had seen better days but still had some life remaining in it. My son and I set about the task of dismantling it for an overhaul. As we worked together on the kitchen floor, I tasted the first fruits of what would become many rewarding times of fellowship while teaching my son about life. As we labored together I experienced the joy of watching him learn the use of a screwdriver and pliers. I laughed at the grease he managed to smear all over his face. He stumbled and bumbled his way through each part of the project but I loved every minute of it.

When our project was completed I plugged the vacuum cord into the wall outlet while my son waited to throw the switch. With a proud smile on his little grease-covered face, he switched it on. As the old vacuum roared to life, in triumph he exclaimed, "Daddy, we did it!"

At that moment I began to realize what fatherhood was all about. To my son it was adventurous but at times frustrating also. To me it was more rewarding than any accomplishment I had experienced in life. It was a type of fellowship that can only be tasted between a parent and child. We had done it together. It was an accomplishment we both shared in; I was the guide and teacher, he was the student. I did not care that he was untrained and unprepared to meet the challenge and he did not fear the challenge knowing that his dad was there to do it with him. He trusted me as a good father to be patient and teach him. I was more than willing to help him because of my sincere love for him. There was no condemnation when he smeared grease over his face and he did not fear rejection when the test of the final product came. He did not see me as a critical judge standing over him during this challenge. He saw me as I wished him to see me, as his Dad. The result was pure joyous fellowship.

This parent - child fellowship is at the core of our heavenly Father's desires. Psalm 149:4a reads:

For the Lord delights in his people. (NLT)

He loves the fellowship of His children. He takes pleasure in teaching us; working with us and helping us succeed. Our success brings Him glory just as a natural child's success brings glory to his or her natural parents. We were created to show His glory. In the process of working towards that end-result He glories in fellowship with us.

It is hard to imagine the great omnipotent creator of the universe taking pleasure working with us on the kitchen floors of our life – but it is true. More than the title of King, Lord and most-High-God, he desires to be known and treated as, Father.

PART TWO

WITH HIM IN HIS SCHOOL

Everyone who comes must come born again by His Spirit as a little child, humble, trusting, and ready to learn and grow naturally. Everyone starts at square one. It just can't work any other way. And that is perfect.

Chapter 4

Growing Up Begins at Birth

I remember wondering what terrible thing my wife, Robin, and I had gotten into after we brought our first child home from the hospital. Nathan was a beautiful baby, but I soon realized that newborns have very different sleeping habits than adults. In particular, he seemed to sleep during the day and stay up crying at night, all night. This was a terrible shock to my system since I had to work days as a carpenter to afford working as a pastor on evenings and weekends.

In spite of the tremendous investment this new person required from us, we loved him dearly and, after a few months of adjustment, even grew to enjoy our service to his nightly needs. One little smile from his baby face made the long hours worthwhile.

By the time our second child, Matthew, our third, Jennifer, and fourth, Sadie, came along, we grew to look forward to the very things we struggled with those first months with baby Nathan.

I didn't require my babies to be perfect and I didn't get angry when they screamed all night. Parents who get angry over that stuff just amaze me. Good parents don't get angry with little babies. Neither does your Father in heaven get angry with His babies. Unfortunately, we often don't see it this way when we enter His kingdom. In the brightness of His perfection we see ourselves as constant failures in need of repeated forgiveness for stupid acts. We tend to look about at the maturity level of more experienced Christians and become frustrated or get our pride tweaked when we can't seem to measure up. It is good to have high standards to emulate. It is bad to forget that they are only standards.

Ultimately, and thankfully, our Father measures us by taking our spiritual age into consideration. He loves His babies just as much as His young-people and the elder children of His house. And of course the younger we are in Him, the more He extends His patience. He knows that growing up in His house, and getting to know Him, begins at birth. And truly we must all begin as newborns in His house.

A fellow named Nicodemus found this truth one evening in a private meeting with Jesus. Let's sit in on their conversation based on the Gospel of John, Chapter 3.

***

"Husband, where are you going at this hour?" called Nicodemus' wife from the rear of the house.

"Out," replied Nicodemus hurrying to find his cloak.

"Out to where?" demanded his wife, "It is dark and near to bedtime. What are you up to Nicodemus?"

"I'm going to find the teacher. The one they call Jesus. I need to speak to him," he replied.

"But Nicodemus, what if someone sees you?" she asked. "Think about your position in this community. You know that this man is considered a traitor. What if someone on the council hears about this? You worked so hard to get a seat on that council. You could lose everything," she warned.

Nicodemus couldn't be swayed from his choice. "It is dark. No one will see me. I will be careful," he muttered passing through the room with his lantern.

"But why must you go at all?" she asked with concern, "He is not even a member of the Pharisees as you are."

Nicodemus paused for a moment to answer, "I must speak to him. Did you not hear of the miracles performed by his hand? With all of the knowledge our council possesses not one of us ever performed a miracle. I must speak to him face to face. I must know..."

"Must know what?" his wife interrupted, "Who knows more than you my husband? You are a teacher and a leader of your people. What can he tell you that you do not already know?"

"I'm not sure. There is just something about this man. He is more than a teacher. I must go to him." Nicodemus said as he cast a gentle smile to his wife.

"Please be careful Nicodemus. I will wait up for you," she replied as she pulled his cloak up tighter to his shoulders as Nicodemus went into the night to find this Jesus.

***

James, startled by a strangely familiar figure coming up the trail, called out softly, "Peter, someone is coming."

"Who is it? Can you make him out, James?" asked Peter.

It suddenly struck James as to why the stranger looked so familiar. "It looks like... no it can't be... yes... it is... it's Nicodemus," he declared.

"Are you kidding? Nicodemus, the Pharisee?" Peter whispered back.

"Yes, look. It *is* him," James said pointing down the hedge-line along the trail.

"What could he want?" Peter wondered aloud, "And why did he wait until now to come?" he asked with suspicion, "James," Peter commanded, "You better run tell the Master."

Following simple greetings, the disciples sat quietly as Nicodemus and the Master spoke.

Nicodemus addressed the Master, "Teacher," he said, "we know that God sent you to teach us. Your miracles are evidence that God is with you."

Jesus replied, "Nicodemus, unless you are born again, you cannot see the Kingdom of God."

"What do you mean?" asked Nicodemus. "How can an old man like me go back into his mother's womb and be born again?"

The disciples listened as the Master Jesus responded with His usual gentle yet straightforward boldness, saying, "Listen to me Nicodemus. With everything I am I tell you that unless you are born again you will never enter the kingdom of God."

***

Everyone Must Begin As A Child

The term, "Born Again," has been used so extensively in society that it is now cliché. The term originates here in the Gospel of John where Nicodemus (a man getting up in years) came to see if Jesus really was who He claimed to be. Jesus' response was that everyone who wanted to enter His Father's kingdom would have to be born again, meaning that we must enter the heavenly Father's kingdom as newborn babies, born this time from His Spirit.

Jesus was telling Nicodemus (who was an accomplished teacher and elder in his community) that he would need to begin again in the Spirit, brought to life inside his spirit and learning everything from the ground up as does a new born baby. This would have been a very difficult and humbling thing for Nicodemus to accept because he had spent his entire life studying to gain knowledge and build prestige as a teacher and leader. Jesus spelled the absolute fulfillment of everything Nicodemus was supposedly working at every day. A new order was unfolding through Jesus. Nicodemus' job was about to become obsolete.

Nicodemus served the old covenant. Jesus was about to cut the new covenant. Nicodemus needed to be completely re-born all the way down to his very spirit. All the rules were about to change! The old tabernacle system of God visiting amongst His people by way of the priests was about to be put away. The new system of God living in every one of His people without the need for human priestly intervention was about to begin. When Jesus told Nicodemus that he most assuredly must be born again as a little child in order to see God, the man was staring straight into the face of the end of his life's work. It was time for Nicodemus to cast aside his prestigious past and enter the kingdom of God as a newborn baby. That is why Jesus gave him the honor of hearing it straightforward. No sugar coating. Jesus basically said, "This is the way through the gate. Take it or you will never see God."

Jesus' words to Nicodemus, though difficult for Nicodemus to hear, were the perfect answer to such a man. Jesus knew that if Nicodemus could not get past this fundamental truth of beginning again as a newborn child, he would never find or understand the kingdom of God. And he would most assuredly not be able to see Jesus as the Son of God. His words to Nicodemus are just as important to each one of us as we come to the gates of God's Kingdom.

And Jesus called a little child unto him, and set him in the midst of them and said, Verily I say unto you. Except ye be converted, and become as little children, ye shall not enter into the kingdom of heaven.
Matthew 18:2-3 (KJV)

If we fail to understand the principle of entering His kingdom as babies we will be constantly frustrated in our efforts to understand what God is doing with us and what He expects from us. Any attempt to enter the gate to God's kingdom as a grown-up is simply pride. No one enters kindergarten as a grown up. No one can enter their new life in Jesus that way either. And that is great news! We don't need to start out as know-it-alls! We can relax and enjoy growing up in our Father's care. Everyone who comes must come born again by His Spirit as a little child, humble, trusting, and ready to learn and grow naturally. Everyone starts at square one. It just can't work any other way. And that is perfect.

Ultimately the Father desires to fellowship with us as mature children. But the path to maturity is a process. The start of this process is infancy. Being an infant in God's kingdom is nothing to be ashamed of. Everyone who is truly His child begins as an infant. And although the Father wishes to fellowship in maturity, He loves His little ones no less. Too often young Christians are led to believe that they must first get good or more spiritually mature before they can experience the Father's fellowship. Nothing is further from the truth. God loves being with His babies.

Babies are wonderful. Even their smell can move a parent's heart to joy. When they arrive they immediately become the focus of a parent's entire life. A parent works for that child, protects that child, provides for that child, and sets great goals and plans for that child. And babies can do no wrong. Our Father in Heaven approaches the care of His newborns much the same way.

I remember my first lesson in the digestive process of a baby. My wife had just finished feeding baby Nathan. She handed him to me while I was reclining on the floor until she could clean up the usual collection of baby food jars and miniature spoons that accompanied every feeding. I promptly began to toss what I dreamed to be my future football-star over my head and watching with glee the surprised expression in his big round eyes. Just them my wife's voice came from the kitchen warning me about shaking up the baby so soon after a feeding. As I turned my head to ask her why, my wonderful first-born son deposited his most recent feeding in my left ear. We laughed for hours and spent the next several days entertaining our friends and family recounting the incident. Neither anger nor disappointment ever entered our minds over the incident. It was to be expected from a newborn. In fact, we enjoyed it and to this day cherish those silly memories. Every one of those little incidents and the endless hours we put into the care of each of our newborns were a form of fellowship with them that we enjoyed totally.

Just as natural newborn children bless parents in the simplest of ways, so we do bless our heavenly Father when we enter His Kingdom as spiritual newborn children. We are His babies. It is His joy to take care of us. We do not need to fear His wrath because of youthful mistakes. Though our ability to fellowship with Him is limited at that point in our new life, He understands and takes joy in our frailty and enjoys our youthful fellowship. Just as a natural parent feels accomplishment and pleasure in caring for a newborn, so does our heavenly Father. Too often we rob Him of these opportunities by losing sight of our position as newborns and by not believing He understands and enjoys us at this age. In doing so, we burden our own souls with unnecessary and unwarranted condemnation. Your Father adores you! Enjoy Him!

In the seventh chapter of his letter to the Roman church, Paul made an incredibly honest confession about his own wrestling with the growing pains of his new life in Jesus. He declared;

> *I have discovered this principle of life—that when I want to do what is right, I inevitably do what is wrong. ...Oh, what a miserable person I am! Who will free me from this*

life that is dominated by sin and death? (But he goes on to reveal what he had come to learn) *Thank God! The answer is in Jesus Christ our Lord ... So now there is no condemnation for those who belong to Christ Jesus."*
Romans 7:21,24-25, 8:1 (NLT)

The Apostle Paul had learned that growing up into maturity and perfection takes time and a lot of help from our Lord. We do not come to maturity by our own abilities, but by the workings of our Lord Jesus who the Bible tells us is the author and finisher of our faith. It is He who leads us as a good shepherd to the fullness of maturity before our Father. Paul came to know that there is no condemnation in the process, only the great grace, mercy and love of a caring heavenly Father and an older Brother who understand our weaknesses. His only desire in this process is that we believe in His fatherhood enough to walk with Him, learn from Him, and live with Him as we grow. From this childlike level of faith he takes us on to perfection, teaching us patiently in His custom-designed school and on to knowing Him perfectly.

Chapter 5

Gaining All by Knowing Him

Edward Jones was left a large inheritance by a long lost relative. Edward was very poor. Years before the death of his relative he moved away to another city, in another state, into a one-room shack with no heat or plumbing. As the Last Will and Testament of his relative was read, Edward's name came out as the inheritor of one million dollars. Those present looked at each other in bewilderment. Edward was not there and no one knew where he had gone. In spite of a long and diligent search by the lawyer assigned charge of executing the estate, Edward was not found. The lawyer faithfully put his one million dollars into the bank for him. In the meantime, Edward was still living in a one-room shack with no heat or plumbing. In reality he was wealthy, but in *knowledge* he was as poor as the guy living in the broken-down shack next to his. The neighbor was dirt poor. Edward was a millionaire. But because of his lack of knowledge, he was in the same place as his penniless neighbor. Poor blind Edward. Well, money isn't everything, but knowing your heavenly Father is. It can mean the difference between seeing Jesus risen or seeing only an empty tomb.

***

Early on Sunday morning, while it was still dark, Mary Magdalene came to the tomb and found that the stone had been rolled away from the entrance. She ran and found Simon Peter and the other disciple, the one whom Jesus loved.
John 20:1,2 (NLT)

Life With Our Father

John moved to the window at the sound of someone running up the path. "Peter look! Isn't that Mary running this way?" he said.

Peter came up next to John at the window. "Yes, it looks like her. What is she shouting?" he asked.

Mary's voice shrieked with indignation, *"PETER! JOHN! HURRY! YOU MUST COME RIGHT AWAY!"*

"Mary, what is it? What has happened?" called Peter.

"Peter, the stone has been moved!" She exclaimed as she burst through the door.

"What stone, Mary? What are you talking about?" asked Peter.

"The stone! The stone that they put at the entrance to His grave! It has been moved! Peter, they have taken the body of our Master!" she declared, her voice now filled with great sadness.

"WHAT! Why would they do this? Where have they taken Him?" demanded Peter.

"I do not know. The stone is lying off to the side and He is gone!" she reported.

"Peter, where are you going?" called John as Peter raced out the door.

"To the grave. I'm going to find out what is going on. Hurry John, we must run!" instructed Peter.

John quickly caught up to Peter and coming to the grave ahead of him exclaimed, "Peter! Come quick! It is just as Mary told us."

Peter came around the last bend to see the grave opening exposed and the huge stone used to secure it rolled to the side. An empty feeling swept through him.

"Did you look inside yet?" asked Peter as he came near to John now standing bewildered near the gravestone.

"I looked but didn't go in. I saw His grave clothes lying there. I just couldn't go in Peter. He is gone," answered John.

Peter didn't hesitate, "I'm going in," he said.

It seemed forever as John waited outside the grave. "Peter, what do you see?" he called quietly, reverently.

Peter replied, "John, come in. I want you to see something."

John slowly entered the rock cave giving his eyes time to adjust to the dim light. "What is it Peter?" he asked.

"There, over there. The burial clothes are here in a pile, but look there, the napkin that was over his face is here," Peter pointed out.

"Yeah, so?" answered a puzzled John.

"Look at it John. Look at how it is folded. It is exactly how He folded His dinner napkin the night we ate with Him," whispered Peter, barely able to breathe with wonderment.

"Yes, you are right. But Peter, I saw Him die... I don't understand. What can this mean? Where is He, Peter? What is happening?" asked John.

"I don't know, John," replied Peter.

"Who took Him, Peter?" asked John.

"I don't know. Maybe..." Peter's voice trailed off as he stared at the folded napkin.

"Maybe what, Peter? What is it?" asked John.

"Nothing John. Nothing. I'm going." Peter replied as he stepped from the cave to return home.

***

Here is an incredible moment in history. Jesus Christ has just fulfilled the age-old prophecy of His resurrection. The tomb is empty. He is risen and gone. Along come two of His very own disciples, men who walked with Him three years prior to His death. But even in the face of an empty tomb, they did not yet understand the plan of the Cross and resurrection. As of yet, they still did not know their Lord or the reason the Father had sent Him. If they had known, they would have been dancing and shouting in that empty tomb. All they saw was an empty grave, so they went home. The empty tomb held no value to them - yet. Soon that empty tomb would mean everything to them because they were about to meet the risen Jesus and finally understand His purpose, and theirs as well.

Through the knowing of Him

> *Grace and peace be multiplied to you in the knowledge of God and of Jesus our Lord; seeing that His divine power has granted to us everything pertaining to life and godliness, through the true knowledge of Him who called us by His own glory and excellence.*
> 2 Peter 1:2-3 (NAS)

Here in 2nd Peter is a great revelation of what is available to us. This scripture states clearly that our Father has already given us *everything* we need to grow and prosper in His life - *by knowing Him.* Everything means *EVERYTHING*.

Knowing Him and His purposes makes all the difference. It is literally the difference between living a life of fullness or a life of confusion and lack. Peter and John missed the glory of that empty tomb because they simply did not yet know Him and His purposes. What is it that you are missing today? What do you lack in the glorious life that God intends for you? Is the problem morality, finances, your marriage, your children, your health, or relationships? What is it that binds you up and keeps you down? Is it confusion, debt, fear, anger or bitterness? Then hear the promise of 2 Peter 1:3! EVERYTHING has been provided for! None of these areas of life or conditions are left out of that promise! No matter how young or old you are in the Lord, provision has already been made for your every need, - body, soul and spirit - through knowing Him.

Our heavenly Father did not sacrifice His Son to hang on a cross only to get us through the door of salvation. The sacrifice of Jesus on the Cross opened the door to *ALL* of the Father and *ALL* of His goodness. Through Jesus we have complete and full access to everything our Father is. Initial salvation, as glorious as it is, is only the starting point of His blessings to us. From there we are called to go on to perfection in Him, lacking nothing! He did not save us only to watch us stand confused in the old empty tombs of our previous life until we die. He desires you to prosper in His life completely.

If this is true, why do so many who call Him their God struggle through life without ever really knowing or experiencing His fullness? How is it that so many can spend a lifetime in a local church, attending church services and Sunday-School classes for years without real growth and lacking hope, joy and peace while trapped in mediocrity? I hate mediocrity in my life. I can't stand the thought of not finishing my race the way my heavenly Father destined me to finish, in fullness. If you hunger and thirst for all of Him, there is hope. You just need to get to know Him! And He makes it simple.

Many new Christians start out with the basic knowledge of salvation and stop right there. They shortchange themselves. In that place, all they have to live on is the thought, "Jesus died for my sins." That's a nice warm feeling that wears thin after a few days of tribulation. You need more to live in true fullness. And there is so much more! All you need to do is press on. But to get it, you must know it is there. With many Christians this is where the trouble begins. They know in their heart that Jesus died for their sins but in daily life they can't understand why they are still wrestling in the pit of failure. In their limited knowledge of the Father and His divine plan, they feel alone and hopeless to face today, even though they are not hopeless. He is always there! ALWAYS! Even if we don't feel it or know it. But, if you don't know it - then you will never feel it. If you don't know His goodness is there, you will never rest in it. It is as the analogy of having inherited one million dollars but not knowing it.

Everything we will ever need when it comes to living and going on to maturity is already on deposit. Through Jesus we have already received an inheritance of fullness. But too often we just don't see it.

Whose fault is this? It is our fault of course! Unlike a rich relative that died and left us money, Jesus did not remain in the grave. He rose again. He does not rely on chance or the efforts of men to find us. He knows where we are and He is constantly calling to us by His Spirit to draw us on to the full inheritance He made available.

Even in our blindness the Father reaches out to us to search on, calling us and drawing us gently by the Spirit to the understanding that there is more. The Father reaches to us through Christians, through the Bible, and into us by His Holy Ghost. Our accountability is simple: all we need to do is look up from our place of despair by faith and say, "yes," to the voice of the Lord. We need only to take those first steps. From there the Father will lead us on.

Look again at the scripture in 2 Peter and notice how we appropriate (bring into our life) what He promised:

> *...his divine power hath given unto us <u>all things</u> that pertain unto life and godliness, <u>through the knowledge of him</u>...* (KJV)

We gain the, "all things," by getting to know Him through our daily life with Jesus, who came to give us a revelation of the Father.

To some, the heavenly Father is a judge that accepts them only on the basis of good or bad. To another, He is a sugar daddy winking at sin and providing a grand life of earthly blessings. And still to others, He is a far and distant God watching us as through a telescope. When we neglect a continuing relationship with our Lord we end up with skewed ideas of our heavenly Father. And of course we live according to those stunted or perverted understandings. Faith, in those who see Him only as a judge, works only if they never sin, and when they do, they fall into a state of condemnation and suffer bitterly from a guilty conscience. They are living the law of the Old Testament. And of course, failing. The ones who see Him as a blind sugar daddy live without regard to any offensive activity and are always in search of more stuff for their treasure houses. Their faith works only until tribulation strikes and then they are sure that God has abandoned them. Those who see Him as a distant God often pass through life in obscurity never experiencing any part of the grand destiny He sets for each of us to experience in our lifetime. We live what we know.

A lack of knowledge and understanding about God can eventually become a box where the soul paces back and forth over the same ground in an endless cycle of repeating the same errors. Eventually a deep weariness sets in causing us to sink hopelessly to the earth below in defeat. Without help from good Christian brothers and sisters, many slip gradually back into the old familiar ways of the flesh, growing callous to anything related to God and His kingdom because God, and the things of God, become too painful to look upon. Others live out their life on earth in a constant state of self-condemnation, working harder to be good and hoping to please God through much work in His kingdom. They often quietly blend into the fabric of a church with the appearance of well-being while inside they are in a constant state of wrestling with old ways and a guilty conscience.

Our Father has given us opportunity to gain everything we need in the knowing of Him through Jesus. What amazing provision. All we need do is get to know Him! And be encouraged! Your Father has already made the way for you.

Chapter 6

The Teacher In Us

My earthly father raised six children working two jobs. By day he was a postman, by night (and most weekends) a carpenter. From my early years I was daddy's carpentry helper, and I loved it. Going off to work with my dad was a never-ending adventure. We would pound nails, cut wood, and pour concrete - every little kid's dream. In all the years I worked at his side I never once doubted our ability to succeed at any job we took on, big or small. I had no fear because I had the master carpenter right at my side.

I can still remember the day he taught me to use a real man-sized handsaw. The saw was as long as I was tall. The board he gave me to cut seemed made of iron and just as heavy. In reality it was one wood step of three we needed to cut to make a set of stairs to a back porch. As I set the saw to the wood I quickly realized that this was not going quite as smoothly as I had seen it done by my dad many times previous. I pushed and pulled and grunted and sweated and got about one quarter inch into the wood before exhaustion set in. My dad, waiting for just that moment, spoke up, "Always use a tool the way it was meant to be used. Never force it." (Hmmmm... I had no idea what he meant. But it sounded right.) "I think the saw is dull. It just won't cut," I replied. "The saw is just fine the way it is," he said, "Try it again but this time only use force when you push it forward. On the pull-back just relax." I did as he suggested and by golly if that saw didn't just miraculously start working. I sawed and sawed and sawed all day. At the end of the day my dad turned the saw upside down and showed me how the teeth of the saw pointed forward and how it only made sense to push on the forward motion and rest on the pull back. It was just that easy. But until the master carpenter instructed me, I struggled to the point of exhaustion.

Imagine having your heavenly Father's very own wisdom, knowledge and understanding living right inside of you. Imagine no more - for on the day of Pentecost it happened! Let's climb the steps to the upper room of Acts, Chapter 2 for a brief glimpse at the event that would change the world.

***

Peter hurried along the path towards the house where the prayer gatherings were being held. Much had changed in seven weeks. Jesus had died right before their eyes. And then, He was there with them again showing the nail scars in His hands. A fresh excitement was in the air. At their last meeting with the Master, He instructed them to wait on Him. And so they waited each day in prayer. Seven weeks since the Master returned from the grave. Nearly two months. Not everyone held on. Many had gone home, not to return. But Peter was determined. He would not miss a day away from his friends, the disciples of Jesus.

"Peter!" exclaimed John, "Come in. We were just talking about the time the Master had you push your boat out to the deep waters and the load of fish you caught that evening. Do you remember?"

"Yes John," replied Peter, "It was amazing."

"Come, sit here with us." invited John.

Peter hugged the others who had come to pray as he moved to an open spot in the upper room next to John. Then quietly they lifted their voices to the heavens just as they had done every day since the Master asked them to wait on Him. For what exactly they were waiting on they did not quite know.

"Peter," John whispered, "Do you hear that?"

"Yes I do." replied Peter. "It's as though the wind is coming right at us from those clouds."

In a flash the room was filled with the sound of the winds. Everyone was awash in a power they had never known. The room exploded with the sound of it. The power washed over them again and again, their knees buckling under the glory of God. Fires kindled over their heads as God's very Spirit poured into them. They opened their mouths to shout glory to God but their words came out in the tongues of other lands. Louder they shouted in the glorious excitement of the room their praises spilling out the windows and doors into the streets. Out from their bellies came shouts of what God had done and people came from all around to the amazing sound.

The Spirit had come. They were given the gift. They were given their teacher. They were given their comforter. They were no longer alone. They would never be alone again. Now they could know their Father perfectly. Now they could walk with Him intimately every day. He was now more than just with them. Now He was *in* them. The church was launched in power. And the Father had His babies back in the throne room with Him.

***

The Patient Teacher

In previous chapters we learned that He wants us to know Him intimately and that we can *gain all by knowing Him*. But Jesus has ascended to the Father and sits at His right hand. What are we to do? How do we learn and grow in this ridiculously evil world without Him here?

As we are about to see, our heavenly Father not only gave us everything we need in knowing Him but He has also provided a step-by-step course to follow, complete with teachers, counselors, fellow students and friends. And it all started right there at Pentecost in those disciples when the Holy Spirit came.

Here is the great glory of being in the Father's school; He did not leave us here alone to hash out our maturity and come to know Him using our own understanding and abilities. Rather, He divinely placed His own Spirit in us as an ever-present personal instructor. Glory! We are not left alone to figure out our own lives. The master teacher is right with us, in us, talking about the Father.

Math class! Oh how I disliked Math class. I was never very good at math. And those tests - investing hours and hours of studying just to get a passing grade. I always envied the kids in class who seemed to just absorb math. It became very obvious to me at a young age that God did not intend for me to serve Him with fractions and logarithms. And believe me, I was not disappointed.

Consider what it would have been like to have your math teacher living inside of you during high school. Even before you walked into your math classroom you would have had everything you needed to succeed in that class. In a flash you could draw on all the knowledge and understanding you needed to survive those grueling tests. You would have never feared studying, doing homework, or taking those big mid-term exams. You would have enjoyed every minute of math class. The math teacher inside you would have been a big comfort.

This is exactly what our heavenly Father gives His children through the giving of the Holy Spirit. The Teacher moves in! He comes to us with everything He knows. It all lives right inside of us by His Spirit. The indwelling Spirit of God carries on the work of Jesus in our lives. He does not speak of Himself but of Jesus, the Father, the Father's desires, and the Father's plans. The Holy Spirit is always there, always teaching, always willing. He does not abandon us in times of trouble or turn a cold shoulder when we stumble. And He does not leave us when we flat out rebel. He is the very essence of our Father and our Lord Jesus. The Holy Ghost is the very spirit of everything gentle, loving and pure. He is the very presence of our heavenly Father leading us on through our school of grace to the fullness intended for us - to the better life of knowing God.

Chapter 7

How We Learn

As a remodeling contractor I often served homeowners who had accumulated much do-it-yourself information from home centers, home maintenance books, home remodeling television programs, and Internet how-to sites. On one occasion, I received a call to do an estimate to complete a large room that a homeowner had started weeks earlier as a do-it-yourself project.

Arriving at the residence I found a pair of frustrated homeowners who had gotten part way into hanging wood paneling before realizing that the guy at the home center had not prepared them for the true technicalities of the work. By the time I arrived the walls looked like waves on the ocean and the panel seams were anything but tight and true. All said and done the job required many hours to undo the work that had been done. In this case a project that would have taken experienced professionals only hours to complete, became a weeklong repair and re-do job. As industrious as the homeowners were, mere knowledge was not enough. They lacked experience.

We have this great heavenly Father who sacrificed His own Son so that we could call Him our dad. We can gain all by getting to know Him and He sent us His very own Spirit to live in us as a teacher to help us know Him fully. So how do we learn? Is it some magical instantaneous supernatural gift? Do we suddenly know all? Don't we wish! Let's see *how* we learn about Him.

We Are Not Animals

Consider a newborn child left in the jungle to learn and grow alone. If the infant somehow miraculously survived, he or she would know only the very basic functions of life: eating, sleeping and survival. To movie writers this is the perfect adventure script, but to a real human child this would be a very meager and unfulfilling way of life. Why? - Because we are not animals. We are eternal beings.

Unlike animals, we are each born with eternity in our souls and we are never satisfied with just survival. We were created for so much more. Engrained in our created being is the need to learn and grow. It is the eternal divine call to learn in the spiritual realm that separates us from the animal creation. And although we learn in very natural ways, our aspirations are eternal. Our learning abilities reach far beyond this natural earth. We can reach up through the cosmos and out into eternity.

The actual process of learning is the same in all of us and functions identically in the spiritual as it does in the natural. Our heavenly Father gave us the ability to learn in both realms.

Rookies and Masters

We learn in the natural by observation and by experience. Information (knowledge) is accumulated by each generation and passed down in verbal, experiential and written form. In school we learn information from instructors, books, audio and video media, computers, etc. We read, hear and observe the experiences of others and gain their discoveries and knowledge. With each new generation there is more knowledge available to be passed on.

During our educational process, and after we graduate from high school or college, we take that knowledge and apply it in our lives and jobs. This is the experiential side of learning.

When someone has worked a length of time in a job using the knowledge they accumulated in school we call them, "experienced," and after a longer season at the job we call them, "professionals," or, "masters," of their trade. These are individuals who have matured in their trade by actually investing, over time, the knowledge they gained into some form of practical experience.

Those who have gained information / knowledge without yet putting it to practical experience are called, *"novices,"* or, *"rookies."* As a novice we often think we know how things ought to be, but lack the completion of our education. Knowledge without practical experiential application is incomplete. We never really know something until we use it or interact with it.

Experiential Knowledge

My sons grew up during the video game revolution. When I was a young man the only games we had were tabletop board games (and that amazing vibrating football field game) One fine day, following endless hours of watching my two sons play a video game, I decided that I would secretly try to learn how to play so I could show them that dad was not so old. After reading all the instruction manuals, I decided that I had learned how to do it and proceeded to give it a try. Late one evening, after my wife and children had gone off to bed, I switched on the game and began to guide the little video game guy through a variety of obstacles. I failed within minutes. Crashed and burned. In frustration, and sleepy determination, I ran that game into the wee hours of the morning and, much to my consternation, I never got anywhere. My little seven and nine year old sons were experts - I was a novice. They had the knowledge mixed with experience. I had only knowledge.

I accumulated all the information I could gain on that game from reading the instruction manual and observing my sons using the game. I knew how the controls worked. I knew the object of the game, the rules, the challenges and even its hidden secrets that were not in the game brochure. In spite of all this information, and holding a thirty-year age edge on my sons, I was only a novice who *"thought"* he knew. I was puffed up with knowledge. I thought I was ready. In reality, all I had was information. I had not really *"learned"* the game because I had not completed my education with practical personal experience. I failed at this simple game because of a lack of true experiential knowledge.

As God's children we often fail for the exact same reason. We get a bunch of knowledge without experience and "think" we know. It is a recipe for failure.

Experiential Knowledge - In The Spiritual Realm

Just as the homeowners were frustrated with their failure at doing-it-themselves, so was I frustrated at my failure with that video game. Each of us, the homeowners and I, made the fatal error of assuming that the information we had gathered by reading and observing was enough. By holding up false expectations of our abilities based solely on accumulated information we both failed.

Failure at a video game or a remodeling project is not a major problem. Failure in life however, is often devastating. Like the homeowner with the do-it-yourself project, we often assume that an accumulation of information on God is enough. But gaining information alone will only serve to puff us up, make us arrogant, and set us up for a fall.

Knowledge puffeth up.
1 Corinthians 8:1b (KJV)

In the natural we learn by observation and experience. The same is true of our learning process in the kingdom of our heavenly Father. In our spiritual school we accumulate information from instructors, books, audio and video resources, etc. We read, hear and observe the experiences of others who know God and thus we gain insight from their knowledge and discoveries about our Lord and our Father. We hear of His character, His plans, His ways, etc. From the Biblical patterns laid out to us in the Old Testament, from the teachings of the Apostles and Prophets of the early church, and by the instruction of today's ministers and fellow saints, we are given countless opportunities and resources to gain information concerning our Lord and heavenly Father. Most importantly He gave us His very Word, the Bible, as the foundational, full, and final word in everything.

From the day of our new birth into His kingdom we enter a spiritual school designed to bring us to fullness and completion in the true knowledge of Him. When we gain information in this school we are expected to take it and apply it into our personal lives and in the work of His kingdom, just as we are expected to invest our natural education in our lives and jobs.

When someone has worked a length of time in God's spiritual kingdom we call him or her, experienced. After a longer season in this service we call them, skilled, or as the Apostle Paul said, "master-builders," as was Paul. These are individuals who have matured in the use of God's word by actually investing the knowledge they gained in practical day-to-day application over a period of time.

Just as is true in the natural world, those who gain information in God's spiritual kingdom without ever putting it to practical use are novices. They lack the completion of their education. Again, knowledge without practical experiential application is incomplete. We never really possess true knowledge of God until we use what knowledge we have been given by the Holy Spirit.

Too often we think the answer to our failures is to gain more information about God or the methods that other Christians are using to overcome similar failures. But the more information we gain without using what we've already been given will only cause us to see the task of perfection as more and more impossible. You cannot skip over the day-to-day lessons of the Holy Ghost. Each lesson leads to another. Each rests upon the previous. To skip over dooms us to a return trip around the training course. And the older you get the harder it is to go back and start again.

If we are to ever gain the fullness of our Father's kingdom, we must come to understand that knowing Him is more than a quick accumulation of scriptural or religious information. The true knowledge of the Father comes from both studying and using what we learn in the relationships and challenges of our life. It is simply not enough to sit in a church, week after week, year after year, listening to countless sermons, reading volumes of Christian books, or even memorizing thousands of scriptures. All of that gaining of information only qualifies us as novices, or as the Apostle Paul declared in Hebrews 5 verses 13 and 14, *"we are as babies."* Paul pointed out that the mature are those who *" by constant use have trained themselves to distinguish good from evil."*

By relying on informational knowledge alone I plunged into that video game with false confidence. This false confidence resulted in failure and frustration when the real test of practical use came into play. The do-it-yourself homeowners fell into the same trap and ended up paying double for their project.

Many of God's children suffer devastation by relying on informational knowledge alone while trying to face the challenges and inevitable trials that come into our lives. They are living on sand and often do not realize it until it is too late.

In the Gospel of St. Matthew chapter 7 verses 24-27, Jesus drew this analogy of the issue of not applying our education experientially,

> *"These words I speak to you are not incidental additions to your life, homeowner improvements to your standard of living. They are foundational words, words to build a life on. If you work these words into your life, you are like a smart carpenter who built his house on solid rock. Rain poured down, the river flooded, a tornado hit— but nothing moved that house. It was fixed to the rock.*
>
> *"But if you just use my words in Bible studies and don't work them into your life, you are like a stupid carpenter who built his house on the sandy beach. When a storm rolled in and the waves came up, it collapsed like a house of cards."* (The Message)

Life is not a math quiz. We can't succeed at it by piling up information. Our relationship to our heavenly Father is not an English test that can be passed or failed. Life is built on experience. Relationship and fellowship with our Father is also built on experience. The more we put action to His words, the more we understand and prosper in His life, and the more we come to be one with Him.

The understanding of this call to, "live our lessons," is critical to the understanding of our maturing process in the hands of our Father. If we fail to see this simple truth we will always fear Him and be running from His arranged lessons. There is no need to fear. He has everything under control. Our part is to believe that He wants to teach us and to do our homework by using what we learn in real life. Our part is to take Him at His Word when He says that He will always be with us and never abandon us. And our part is to face each test with faith in His unwavering integrity, that He will turn everything to the good and teach us His way of seeing life. You can trust Him to lead you through each of life's lessons and you will never be disappointed in the end.

Chapter 8

Divine Teaching Techniques

"I can't get up the curb, dad. Will you lift my bike for me?" asked Jennifer my five-year-old daughter. I was walking alongside her as she rode her new training bicycle. When we came to that street curb she stopped cold. With a gentle smile I knelt down next to her and with my hand on her shoulder said, "Jennifer, you can do it." As I stepped back a few feet, my daughter grabbed that little bike (which was up to her neck) and smoothly lifted it up over the street curb. When she finished she spun around and with a big smile on her face and declared, "I did it Dad! I did it all by myself!" Hopping back on her bike she gasped, "Lets go tell Mom."

Most young children would rather run and hide from difficulties than face them and learn from them. Good parents, however, know that the greatest opportunities to teach their children are in the tough challenges children face growing up. The best of parents not only recognize this fact but also use it constructively by creating and overseeing controlled and safe obstacles for their children to overcome and learn from.

At a very early age an infant's parents take great pleasure placing their child upright at one end of the room while waiting at the other end of the room with open arms. While the child stares in wonderment, the parent calls to the child to convince the infant to take its first steps. In this very simple act these parents accomplish the most basic of parental duties by setting up opportunity for their child to face a challenge and overcome it.

As a child grows, good parents wisely create greater and more difficult obstacles for their child to face and overcome.

With each new challenge the child matures in knowledge, understanding and wisdom, and grows increasingly confident in his or her own abilities as well as becoming confident in the love of the parents. If a child is blessed with parents who are willing to carry on this level of training throughout the child's growing years then he or she is much better equipped to face the challenges of adult life with success.

As my children grew I gave them one challenge after another in order to help them develop an understanding of the value of working hard and to build character in them concerning teamwork and consideration of others. One of the challenges I gave them was to enroll them in athletics at a very young age. My girls loved cheerleading and track, and my boys loved wrestling and football. The value of these challenges hit home to me one fateful day years later.

After completing his high school and college education, my eldest son pursued a career in law enforcement. It is a never-ending delight for me to hear of his exploits in crime fighting. And it is a pleasure to watch him demonstrate the character he learned from the honorable people of his life. On one occasion he told me of a dark evening as he attempted to stop a man for a simple traffic violation. The man bolted in his vehicle, drove a short way, jumped from the car and ran on foot. When my son caught up to the obviously intoxicated man, the guy wheeled around, grabbed my son's shoulder radio and struck him on the head with it causing it to break into pieces. My son was left without a radio behind a shopping center wrestling a dangerous character. Using a move he learned in high school wrestling my son subdued the man, placed him under arrest and waited for backup. Cut up and bleeding, he finished out his shift and went home. When I asked him if he got angry with the man when he hit him with the radio, he very matter-of-factly said, "No. I was just trying to keep him from hurting himself." What a very proud moment that was for me. In the face of hatred, he simply cared about helping the very one that was trying to hurt him. What greater love has any man than this? It made my day to hear him say those words. The athletic challenges I gave him growing up, and the coaches who taught him in those sports, helped protect him that night. The exposure I gave him to honorable people in the house of the Lord over the years created a tender heart in a man who put his life on the line for a wayward soul on a dark night. That is what it's all about.

Hearing such stories of progress in my children's lives just thrills me. Our heavenly Father is no less delighted with our progress and the fruit it bears in our lives, and, He is a faithful father when it comes to teaching us. Just as I had given my children opportunity to face tough challenges physically and socially, our heavenly Father presents us with challenges that are designed for our maturing in His house. These challenges come in different forms but all are intended to bring us to the fullness of knowing Him; and by knowing Him we gain a fullness of life for ourselves.

The learning opportunities arranged for us by our heavenly Father become experiential during our daily life. In the arena of life He teaches and transforms us into His image by encouraging us to stand up and step out in faith as little children learning to walk. He gives us opportunity to face tribulation so that we might find His face and grow in strength. He teaches us that, "we can do it," by pressing us into new experiences and letting us tough them out. All of these opportunities for growth are intended to prepare us for life ahead and ultimately to ensure our completion in maturity. This process is the earmark of true sons and daughters of God. He works it in us for the same reasons an earthly parent puts controlled obstacles before us. They are expressions of love and as such are not to be feared.

> *We can rejoice, too, when we run into problems and trials, for we know that they help us develop endurance. And endurance develops strength of character, and character strengthens our confident hope of salvation.*
> Romans 5:3-4 (NLT)

Too often we wrestle with this truth and fail to see God as our good Father working to teach us how to survive and prosper in this life and the life to come. I lived years into my new life as a Christian with the fruit of this misconception. For years after becoming a Christian I heard countless speakers and read volumes of books that taught me; how things should be, how things are, how things will be in the future, what to do and what not to do, as well as thousands of methods covering everything from how to prosper financially, to saving the entire world. But no one ever explained to me that I was in a school and the challenges I wrestled with were actually carefully chosen controlled opportunities for me to face with my Father at my side. At the time I saw these challenges as something only to endure and get delivered from. I spent countless days in prayer asking Him to rescue me or take the problems away rather than facing them with faith in His fatherly overseeing presence. On more than a few occasions I cried out as did the disciples on the boat in the storm, "Lord where are you are? Are you going to let me be destroyed?" By not understanding His teaching methods, I thought I was being abandoned, or worse that He was angry with me and would not respond until I became a better Christian.

Until I understood the long-term purposes of His teaching techniques, and came to believe that He loved me and was in total control, I was never able to rest. On the contrary I was constantly filled with fear of loss, failure, and destruction. At that time, all of my Bible studies revolved around survival and escape techniques. Unfortunately, this desperate, fearful basis of studying opened me up to any teaching that promised prosperity and romanticism. These human centered doctrines only served to steer me further from the simple truth that my heavenly Father had already given me everything I needed to live and grow into the batter life He had planned for me. It was years before I came out of that error and began to realize that tribulations and trials were not something to be feared, but rather were divine appointments prepared to help me learn about the love and life of my Father's kingdom and the glory of the Lord Jesus. Eventually I came to understand that He was not going to rescue me out of every little tribulation and challenge that came my way, but rather expected me to do my best in them, learn from Him by passing through each one *with Him* and then on to victory in Him.

We have nothing to fear in any challenge or tribulation that comes our way. The Apostle Paul, after finding this simple truth through years of experience, declared in his letter to the Roman church chapter 5, verses 3- 5 that, *"he came to glory in tribulation because he had learned that the tribulation and challenges worked to fill him with a greater measure of life."* At the end of his life on the earth, Paul was at complete rest, ready to move on, and prepared to continue in eternity full of his heavenly Father's knowledge. His work on earth was done, his training for eternity complete. School was ending. Graduation time had arrived for him.

Believe in something better! Your heavenly Father has a great plan for you and you can trust Him to teach you all along the way.

Chapter 9

Learning that "We Can Do It"

Have circumstances ever pressed you so hard that you were sure you couldn't go one more day? I had a season like that a while ago. I was in process of buying a new home for my family. We had already sold our previous home and, with full assurance from the lending company of a closing date on the new home, had moved in lock, stock and barrel. What a fool I was. You can guess what happened next.

Just before closing, the lender discovered that the new house relied on well water rather than city lines. A complete water test was mandatory. The closing date was pushed back a month. The seller started getting anxious. Finally, the water issue was resolved and a new closing date was set. But now the age of the septic tank became an issue. Again the closing date was postponed. The seller flipped. They demanded we vacate the house immediately. Me, my wife and our four children had nowhere to go.

I was praying desperately day and night for my heavenly Father to intervene. The pressure was building but I was determined to stay calm and wait on the Lord for an answer. And then, when the closing date was delayed once again for a paperwork issue, I just folded. I had had enough. I opened my mouth and out came these words, "God better do something right now today because I can't take this one more day!" I said this to one of our close friends. All she said in response was, "Oh-oh, you're in trouble now." She was right.

Guess what I learned from that stupid outburst; I learned that indeed I could do it one more day. In fact, I learned that I could do it seven more days because that is exactly how long my Father let me sit until the actual closing. Looking back on it now I can laugh. But it was hell going through it. In the end, I treasure what He taught me by letting me go through that tribulation. I learned that I could hold on and trust Him and that I can do anything my Father puts in front of me to face.

One day, after many days of walking with His disciples, Jesus sent His men out alone to learn that they could do it. Here is their exciting experience based on the account given us in the Gospel of Luke, Chapter 10.

***

After these things the LORD appointed other seventy also, and sent them two and two before his face into every city and place, whither he himself would come. ... Go your ways: behold, I send you forth as lambs among wolves. ... Carry neither purse, nor scrip, nor shoes: and salute no man by the way. ... And heal the sick that are therein, and say unto them, The kingdom of God is come nigh unto you.
Luke 10:1,3,4,9 (KJV)

    The morning sun was already hot on their backs as Andrew and James dipped into the well for a drink. "Hey, Mark, Jacob. Which way are you guys going?" Andrew called seeing them approach.

"We're going south. How about you?" replied Mark.

"We're going south too. We'll walk awhile with you," offered Jacob.

"Can you believe this?" asked Mark with a forward wave of his arm.

"Believe what, Mark?" asked Andrew.

"What he told us to do! Didn't you hear him? We are supposed to do things that only he has done! I have never healed the sick!" exclaimed Mark.

"Yeah, I was thinking about that too. I must admit that all this makes me a little nervous. I've never done anything like this before," noted Andrew.

"Me either," said Jacob, "What does he expect of us?"

"I don't know, but I trust him. Hey, this is our road. We'll see you guys later. God be with you," said Mark reaching out his arms to bid his friends farewell.

"And God be with you," replied Andrew and James.

***

Andrew lifted his face after brushing the dust from his sandals to see Mark and Jacob back at the well where they had left them a month earlier. "Look, there are Mark and Jacob," he said pointing up the road, "Hurry, let's see how they did since we left them last month. Hey, Mark, wait up," he called waving his arms.

Still running to the well James began to call out, "Mark, Jacob, you should have been there. I spoke to a blind man in the Master's name and his eyes opened up right in front of us!"

"We saw the same things," yelled Mark catching James in his arms as he arrived at the well. "In one little town we cast out a demon from a woman who had been insane since childbirth. When we spoke His name the demon threw the woman to the ground and came out of her with a horrible scream. The woman stood up and went away rejoicing!" he reported.

"And in another town we healed two lepers in His name," added Jacob.

"Hey, do you remember how frightened we were when He first told us to go?" asked Andrew.

"Yes. When we entered the first town my hands were shaking. I didn't know how to begin but then I remembered watching Him, and it all fell into place. We did it! Just as he said," exclaimed Mark.

"Come on, let's run and find the Master. We need to tell Him what happened," said Jacob.

***

You Can Do It

Can you imagine being one of those seventy disciples standing before Jesus as he sent them out on this ministry journey? I'm confident that few if any of them had much considered going out on their own to minister in this way. None had any experience at ministry other than watching Jesus, and he wasn't going with them. What an incredible challenge He laid before them. You probably could have heard a pin drop in the sand after He spoke. But they trusted Him and obeyed. Two by two they departed, with no money or food, not knowing where they would sleep, how they would be received, or how well they would perform. They stepped out into one of God's famous teaching events. And they learned that in Christ they could do it.

Of all the things my earthly father gave me, I most appreciate the, "I-can-do-it," ideal that he instilled in me by diligently creating and overseeing controlled challenges. Being the son of a carpenter presented many such opportunities from learning to use a handsaw on a big hunk of wood to later in my career plotting the layout of a complete home addition. All along the way, he proved to me that I could do it if I just set my hand to it and trusted him to be there for me.

In my early years as a young carpenter my duties were limited to whatever I could do safely; running for tools, sitting on the opposite end of a board my father was cutting, etc. As I grew, my father passed on greater opportunities for me to face and learn from. I learned to trust my dad when he said I could do it and learned to trust his judgment when he gave me a task or a challenge to face. I came to realize that if he gave me a task, then he had already determined it to be safe and that I was able. With this confidence in his care and judgment, I learned to rely on his direction and not fear the challenges.

With that foundational training I eventually grew to enjoy the challenges and became willing to face and overcome even the most difficult construction projects. By the time I reached my early twenties I could design and build a project from the ground up without concern over the difficulties of it or fear of failure. From the simple opportunities that my father arranged, I continuously gained in life and success until I reached the fullness of the opportunities that the trade offered. Because of my father's willingness to invest his time and knowledge into my life, and my faith in him, I eventually gained great success in the building and remodeling trades.

Our heavenly Father works much the same way in His efforts to teach us that we can do it. From the point of our salvation He begins to set challenges in front of us that are measured in difficulty by what we are able to handle. In the beginning He teaches us the basics of how to stand up and take our first steps in our new life; teaching us not to fear falling and constantly calling to us with open arms to draw us on into each challenge. As we grow He arranges and permits greater challenges to come our way. Each is a lesson and a test of our maturity. And with each test passed we are given greater opportunities to grow in His knowledge and character.

Just as my earthly father placed a saw in my hand when I was so very young, so does our heavenly Father place new challenges in our path to cut through. These challenges almost always seem big and impossible to us. In the young years of our spiritual life we usually respond the same as I did as a young boy looking down on a thick piece of lumber that needed cut. We feel so small in the face of these challenges that the only words we can muster are, "I can't do it." Our heavenly Father's response is always, "Yes, you can. You can do it. I'm right here. I will not leave you."

I can do all things through Christ (Jesus) which strengtheneth me.
Phil 4:13 (KJV)

Our part in this school of challenges is to pick up the toolbox (the Word of God) and begin in childlike faith. The worst decision we can make when faced with a challenge is to sit down and do nothing or run in frustration or fear. In Part 3 of this book titled, Run-Aways, we'll discuss the tragedies that befall those who make this type of decision in the face of opportunities and challenges.

Facing Tribulations

Another thing my earthly father did for me as I grew up in his house was to let me face most of my foolish self-created tribulations like a man. On more than a few occasions he purposefully withheld his intervention to let me learn. I must admit, I was really ticked off at him at the time, but now of course I am very grateful. On one occasion, his wisdom of withholding rescue worked to teach me one of the greatest lessons of my life.

Most young boys hold dreams of owning a cool car. I was eighteen. I was shopping for a car in preparation for college. I had money for a car that was burning a hole in my pocket. My father and I traveled from car lot to car lot in search of the perfect used car for my purposes. After searching for a while my father spotted a big, boxy, ugly-brown, four-door that he counseled me was the best buy and suited for my travel needs.

I, however, had spotted a flashy bright yellow foreign sports car that I immediately became transfixed by. As my father and I discussed the two cars, he gently told me that it was my choice, but also warned me that I was going to regret passing up the big, boxy, ugly-brown, four-door. But all I could think about was the joy of zipping around campus in that beautiful sports car. I ignored my father's counsel and gleefully bought the little yellow car.

Sometime before the ink dried on the new registration papers, the car's engine blew. After sinking hundreds of dollars into repairing the engine, the specially designed high performance mega-dollar muffler cracked. Before the end of my first year of college that beautiful flashy sports car was rusting out so badly that parts were falling off and I had to carry two batteries and a battery charger to go more than fifty miles.

One day, after I had given the car away for a few hundred bucks, my father pointed out a car driving by our home. It was the big, boxy, ugly-brown, four-door looking as good as it did on the lot the day I passed it up for the idea of driving the sports car.

My father never said a word. He only looked at me and smiled one of those smiles that say, "I told you so."

During the months that my beautiful sports car was transforming into a rolling wreck my father never stepped in to rescue me as he had done in similar situations when I was younger. He realized that the time had come for me to grow up and learn how every decision I made from that day forward would either bring me life or end in death. And, that whatever decision I made, I would have to face the consequences myself as an adult.

That was a very traumatic lesson in my young life and, while I was going through it, I hated every minute of it. My father's lack of quick rescue left me feeling neglected and rejected. At the time I didn't see his actions as love but now, as I am a father myself, I understand and appreciate his determination to not rescue me. I realize now that he knew the experience would be tough and costly but it would not destroy me. He knew I could handle it and survive, and therefore he permitted it to run its full course. He was well able to step in and put a quick fix on the situation. Through his decision to let me face it to the end and work through it, I learned accountability and the value of wise counsel. In the long run these lessons were far more valuable than having or losing a car. Years later I had opportunity to use the exact same lesson with my middle son, Matthew.

Matt is truly a chip-off-the-old-block. After landing a good job out of high school he went right out and bought a shiny used sports car. Within a year the engine blew and he was left with a car loan without a working car. It was tough withholding my hand of rescue but it worked its lessons just at it had by my father before me. Matt faced his situation with integrity, learned his lesson, and did not repeat it.

My heavenly Father has used the same teaching techniques on many occasions during my time in His school. In my early years as a pastor I was battered by a decade of constant tribulations. In each storm the Lord waited until just the right moment to step in and rescue me. Being very young in the ministry these events always shook my heart and I wrestled constantly with questions about why the Lord did not rescue me when I called and why He let me face it to the end. But as time passed, and more seasons of tribulation came and went, I came to realize that I was no longer so easily moved by tribulation. As tough as those seasons were, they taught me how to survive and thrive while facing a certain level of tribulation. I learned better how to pray, how to pull my family together, and, how much I needed my church friends.

If my heavenly Father had jumped in and done a quick fix in those seasons, I would still be easily beaten and bruised to this day. If He had ended the pressure too quickly, I would never have had opportunity to draw as close to my friends and learn of God's strength in prayer and fellowship. And I would have missed the opportunity to learn of His grace, which is always enough for us in every situation. By permitting me the opportunity to face it to the end, He made it possible for me to get closer to Him as a child in need. In the end, the real lesson was that together, He and I could face anything.

Of course, we are never alone in our tribulations. When I refer to Him letting us, "face it to the end," I mean that He lets us walk into and through the tribulation with Him, and then out the other side with Him.

The whole purpose of tribulation is to cause us to search Him out, to find His thoughts and His ways in these experiences, to use the knowledge we already have - thus making it experiential. And all this is to perfect us in His ways so that we can fellowship with Him as His adult children and that we might enjoy a truly full life, a better life by knowing Him.

Tribulation was what caused the disciples to cry out in fear during the storm on the Sea of Galilee. They did not yet know God or His care for their safety. If they had known, they would have rested. This is the value of pressing on in the school of our Father. It brings us to the point of perfect peace and rest.

Dear brothers and sisters, when troubles come your way, consider it an opportunity for great joy. For you know that when your faith is tested, your endurance has a chance to grow. So let it grow, for when your endurance is fully

developed, you will be perfect and complete, needing nothing.
James 1:2-4 (NLT)

Chapter 10

Fatherly Discipline

There is nothing like an old-time, wood-plank-floored corner store. We had one directly across the street from my childhood home. My parents called it, Steve's Store, because a guy named Steve owned it. But to every kid on the block it was wonderland. The shelves were lined with rows and rows of glass jars filled with every delectable candy goody and trinket a ten-year-old child could imagine. And I had a big imagination. Of particular interest to me was one small hand-crank vending machine situated right at the entrance to the store. In that little glass globe were dozens of tiny plastic army men. For just a few dollars I could add a complete platoon of mini-combatants to my backyard battlefield. I REALLY wanted those army men.

Unfortunately, a few dollars may as well have been a few hundred dollars back then. But every day I would faithfully run over to Steve's Store, press my little nose up against the glass and dream. It would have been best if I had left it as a dream. But... I just really wanted my army!

One day after weeks of dreaming I decided to start scrounging around the house for loose change. I flipped cushions and dug behind car seats. I came up with enough to buy one army man. I raced to the store, dropped the coins in the slot, grabbed my new one-inch warrior and ran gleefully to the back yard to start my war. But a one-man army doesn't cut it. I needed more. My little brain started plotting like a seasoned field general. Then it dawned on me! My dad had some coins in wrappers in his cabinet that he had shown me just awhile back. He had instructed me to not touch them. But who would know? There were five other kids in the house to blame.

As it turned out, the coins were sealed collector proofs. You can only imagine what happened next. Let's just say that I didn't sit a lot for the next couple days. Ouch. But guess what? I learned not to take other people's belongings. Real fast.

Soon after becoming newborns in our Father's kingdom we all face the realization that there is a part of us that would rather follow the old ways of living - *a big, big part.*

Everyone likes the image of a cuddly warm-hearted heavenly Father who never gives out spankings or raises his voice. This is a wonderful romantic idea but ultimately very flawed. The problem with this picture is that the cuddly warm Father must be a father to rebellious unruly children. On the other side of the spectrum is the image of a distant mean angry father who takes pleasure in afflicting his children and watching them suffer. Neither of these concepts comes close to the heart of our heavenly Father.

A good father takes no pleasure in doling out chastisement, but rather, out of love for the child's future, he knows it is necessary. A good father never executes chastisements out of personal anger or discomfort. Instead, the chastisements are carefully chosen to tutor a child in life for the child's own good. Imperfect earthly fathers often strike out when the actions of a child annoy or anger the parent personally. I once watched in agony as a parent arbitrarily struck out at an excited child who had interrupted his dad's TV program to tell him about something he needed for school. This is not chastisement. It is more like impatient selfishness.

True chastisement, which comes from our heavenly Father, revolves around the concept of nurturing. Nurturing defined is: to support, train up and educate during stages of growth. Nurturing assumes a long-term commitment of investment in a child and for the child's good. The execution of our heavenly Father's chastisement works from such a commitment. His chastisements are given out according to His commitment to our eternal lives. They are meant to preserve us today and prepare us for the long haul here on earth and, inevitably, to draw us closer to Him. And the closer we come to Him the more life we will experience in fullness. Our heavenly Father's chastisements are intended to change us for the good.

The process of changing is referred to in the scriptures as: putting off the old and putting on the new. This is the gradual casting away of our old ways of living and thinking and replacing them with the new ways of life and new thinking processes of our Father's kingdom.

Ephesians 4:17-24 states:
With the Lord's authority I say this: Live no longer as the Gentiles do, for they are hopelessly confused. Their minds are full of darkness; they wander far from the life God gives because they have closed their minds and hardened their hearts against him. They have no sense of shame. They live for lustful pleasure and eagerly practice every kind of impurity. But that isn't what you learned about Christ. Since you have heard about Jesus and have learned the truth that comes from him, throw off your old sinful nature and your former way of life, which is corrupted by lust and deception. Instead, let the Spirit renew your thoughts and attitudes. Put on your new nature, created to be like God—truly righteous and holy. (NLT)

The Need of Discipline

It would be nice if we could learn and change simply by hearing the right way to live and doing it without fail. We all know this is far from reality. Our tendency to miss the mark is the fruit of both our fallen nature that we inherited from the sin of the first man, Adam, and having lived part of our life outside of our Father's house. The habits and tendencies of that old life become ingrained in us. And they don't leave willingly.

During our time before salvation, we learned in great detail how to keep our flesh happy. Our entire decision making process in that realm was governed by our pleasure levels. If something looked fun or enjoyable we went after it. If something appeared unrewarding or possibly painful to us, we avoided it. This is the natural earthly and sensual way of making decisions.

From Adam we inherited the lusts of the eyes, the lusts of the flesh and the pride of life. Or in other words, what looked good, felt good, and glorified us personally. Before we are saved we are like a child jumping at the chance for a piece of candy but refusing a plate of vegetables. The vegetables offer nutrition and health. The candy offers nothing but sensual pleasure. The vegetables are the choice of wisdom and life. The candy is the choice of temporary enjoyment. Inevitably, when given the choice, the natural child will choose the candy. After years of living for our own gratification, our decision-making processes become rooted in these habits of temporal carnal pursuit.

As new believers coming into the Father's kingdom, we function in this sensual, earthly, carnal-thinking, decision-making process until we learn differently. This is normal and expected. This is what Jesus was talking about when He told Nicodemus that everyone must be born again to enter the kingdom of God. At the point of new birth all of those old carnal ways of thinking and making decisions become worthless. All the rules have changed. By the salvation of Jesus Christ our lives become eternally based. Our new thinking must revolve around heavenly things rather than the things of the earth. Our decisions must be determined by eternal values rather than temporary gratification. The problem arises when we face the reality that those old habits of thinking do not magically disappear at the point of new birth. Not only do they not disappear but they fight to hang on.

Paul spoke of this war between his flesh and his new spirit in his letter to the Romans the seventh chapter:

> "...I do not understand what I do. For what I want to do I do not do, but what I hate I do...in my inner being I delight in God's law; but I see another law at work in the members of my body, waging war against the law of my mind and making me a prisoner of the law of sin at work within my members. What a wretched man I am! Who will rescue me from this body of death? Thanks to be God – through Jesus Christ our Lord!" (NIV)

Paul was describing the powerful war his flesh (and it's habits) had waged against the new way of life that salvation had brought to him.

It is through informational learning (the word of God) mixed with His chastisement (correction) that we learn to put off the old ways of living and thinking and put on the new ways of thinking and decision making necessary for prospering in His new life.

Chastisement is the gentlest method the Father can use to change our way of thinking. By permitting us to undergo controlled hardships, the painful fruit of carnally based decision-making is highlighted and thus we gain quick understanding of how dangerous carnal choices can be. By permitting affliction to hit our souls, He gets us to respond properly. In other words, He makes it more painful to think and live carnally than to think and live spiritually. And even though we do not like any part of chastisement, it is ultimate love from a caring Father. This is the earmark of those who are truly His children. This process is found only in true children of God. As Paul stated in his letter to the Hebrews, "He chastises those He loves."

This process of learning to think spiritually is critical. As stated in the eighth chapter of Paul's letter to the Romans, *"To be carnally minded is death; but to be spiritually minded is life and peace."* (KJV) Chastisement from our heavenly Father is for our own good so that in time we will gain the peace and fullness of life that righteousness (being right and living His ways) brings.

The Spirit of His Chastisement

We have already discussed the value of knowledge and experience to the development of our new lives. Chastisement is the second hand of our heavenly Father's nurturing process, and is no less necessary or valuable than the knowledge-by-experience process.

Unfortunately many believers fall to the mistake of despising chastisements, which the Apostle Paul warned of in his letter to the Hebrews. If we fail to see chastisement as another part of the heavenly Father's love, we will despise it when it comes our way and rebel against it. And if we refuse to accept chastisement, we disqualify ourselves from being sons and daughters of the heavenly Father.

Natural children cannot choose their earthly parents. We are all born into that position. Being a child of God, however, is an adoption-like choice that we are free to accept or refuse.

Our choice is made clear by our willingness to be under His authority. Part of being under His authority is bowing to and accepting His instructions *and* chastisements. If we despise His discipline and refuse to be chastised by Him, we are actually declaring that we refuse the authority of His fatherhood.

> *"My child, don't make light of the Lord's discipline, and don't give up when he corrects you. For the Lord disciplines those he loves, and he punishes each one he accepts as his child." As you endure this divine discipline, remember that God is treating you as his own children. Who ever heard of a child who is never disciplined by its father? If God doesn't discipline you as he does all of his children, it means that you are illegitimate and are not really his children at all. But God's discipline is always good for us, so that we might share in his holiness. No discipline is enjoyable while it is happening—it's painful! But afterward there will be a peaceful harvest of right living for those who are trained in this way.*
> Hebrews 12:5b-8 & 10b-11, (NLT)

In these days of relaxed family discipline, I have witnessed children absolutely and often violently despise the sincere correction of their parents. It is a very sad affair. I am so very grateful to my heavenly Father for teaching me the love in chastisement at a very young age and for helping me pass it on to my own children. My youngest daughter, Sadie, is very creative, energetic and social. And she, like all my children, got herself into hot water on more than a few occasions. But every time I corrected her, no matter how severely, she got right up afterward, hugged me, thanked me for being a good dad, and jumped right into repairing the damage her choices and actions caused. She is always moving to maturity. This is exactly what our reaction should be to our heavenly Father's corrections. When we respond this way, He takes us right on to maturity and we gain opportunity to be closer to Him.

Chapter 11

The Parts of Chastisement

All scripture is given by inspiration of God, and is profitable for doctrine, for reproof, for correction, for instruction in righteousness: That the man of God may be perfect, thoroughly furnished unto all good works.
2 Timothy 3:16-17 (KJV)

    When my two sons were infants we lived in a poorly heated third floor apartment. Our main heat source was an old gas fired freestanding furnace that jutted out into the middle of our living room. When it was lit, the sides and face of the unit became dangerously hot to the touch. With two small children playing within inches of the furnace it was a constant concern.
    Realizing the danger to the children, my wife and I set about the process of warning the children concerning getting too close to the furnace. Again and again we offered reproofs concerning the results of touching the metal sides to that furnace. But in spite of our verbal warnings the children continued to press the boundaries of safety. Finally a choice had to be made about taking them into a more severe discipline that would drive the point home in their young hearts. The season of gentle reproofs had ended.
    On the next occasion of their journey near the furnace I grudgingly applied a more sever discipline. A minute later, once the tears had dried, the boys went happily back to their toys on the living room floor and never went near the furnace again.
    Though tough love is never enjoyable, it is truly mercy. Our gentle reproofs were mercy and our eventual rebuke was

mercy. I would have been happier if the boys would have accepted the first level of mercy but in the end they were both saved from a possible serious burn and lifelong scar. Even more importantly they learned that they should never touch anything hot. Though this loving chastisement they were preserved and prepared for the future.

I must admit that I really never liked being chastised and I always dreaded chastising my children. But few things in my life have impacted me as positively as my earthly father's chastisements. In fact, there have been many times in my adult life that I wished my dad had been more diligent chastising me when I was growing up. Most of what I wrestle with today could have been squashed in me at a young age with a few well-placed chastisements. But hindsight is always twenty-twenty and I'm eternally grateful to my dad for his tough love. He taught me how to chastise my own children with love and patience.

Why is it important for us to understand chastisement on our journey to knowing our God? Because He uses it to teach us the difference between what is life and what is death. He chastises those He loves.

> *"My child, don't make light of the Lord's discipline, and don't give up when he corrects you. For the Lord disciplines those he loves, and he punishes each one he accepts as his child."*
> Hebrews 12:5-6 (NLT)

If we don't understand chastisement we can easily become discouraged and often fall into bitterness towards our Father. This should never be our course in the face of such a gentle God.

The term, chastisement, usually conjures up images of a spanking or corporal punishment of some form. True chastisement, however, involves three progressive steps. What we know as spanking is referred to as, rebuke, in the scriptures. Rebuke is only one of the steps of chastisement. There is also reproof and correction. This process is part of learning about life with our Father. And whether we like it or not - it is a part of who He is. And, after thirty-five years of being His son, I am grateful for it.

Reproof - the Warning

The beginning of chastisement is reproof. Reproof is that step in which a child is warned. When a good parent sees a child headed into trouble, the parent sends out a gentle warning in an attempt to correct the child's course. The warning usually sounds like; "You better not do that. You'll get hurt," or "Be sure to look both ways before you cross the street." A reproof can also carry some form of evidence to convince the child further such as; "If you don't brush those teeth you'll get cavities and need to visit the dentist." This added evidence spells out the error and the disastrous end of the error. This offering of warning and evidence is the essence of reproof.

The reproof step of chastisement is the opportunity we get to avoid the next step in chastisement, and of course the discomfort between steps one and two increases significantly. But if we respond humbly to reproof, and learn from it, we need go no further.

An honest older Christian who has matured well in the Lord will testify of the heavenly Father's faithfulness to have always offered a reproof warning before they fell into the next steps of chastisement. One of the first questions I ask someone who comes to me for help after getting themselves into a big mess is, "When in this event did the Holy Spirit warn you to stop?" Amazingly, through thirty years of asking that question, every person has been able to tell me exactly when they were warned.

Our heavenly Father is a very, very longsuffering father. He would much rather we listen-up and obey before we force his hand to take us to the next step. But we don't always do that, alas, we all face step two; rebuke. Some of us will face it a few times, some of us many, many times. Ouch.

Rebuke - the Tough Love

Young boys seem ever in need of life-saving rebukes. I was no different. One of my most dangerous activities was running across the street without looking both ways. When my dad caught me doing it he would give me a good pop on the behind to stop me in my tracks. As it turned out, his rebukes would save my life.

One day as I raced out between two parked cars I suddenly remembered that I was supposed to look both ways. Just at that moment, as I slowed my pace, I came face-to-face with the chrome trim of a big baby-blue car streaking down the street. I hit the side of it face first and bounced back onto the curb. I was beaten and bruised, and gave my poor mom a near heart attack, but I survived. Who knows what would have become of me without dad's rebukes.

A rebuke can be defined as a severe reproof. Unlike a reproof, however, a rebuke does not offer much room for personal choice of direction. While reproof is an opportunity to correct yourself, a rebuke is an *imposition* placed on us by someone more powerful. A reproof warns us of impending disaster, while a rebuke cuts us off from going any further by blasting us to attention. A reproof offers us evidence in an effort to convince us to change while a rebuke offers no explanation until after the pain of the rebuke is felt. Reproof and rebuke are both forms of mercy. Both are meant to keep us from getting the fullness of disaster that we could face.

Correction - the Adjustment

Correction is the third step of chastisement. Unlike reproof and rebuke, correction is a process that works to straighten us up and readjust our path. Correction is what we receive at the conclusion of reproof and / or reproof and rebuke.

A good analogy of how correction works is that of a man walking blindly to the edge of a cliff with his friend watching him. As the man walks towards disaster his friend begins crying out warnings (reproof) long before he reaches the edge. If the man ignores the cries of warning, his friend races to him to tackle him (rebuke) before he goes over the edge. As the man stands, his friend brushes the dirt from his clothes, rubs the pain from his bruised knees, and says, "Now – turn around and go this way." (Correction)

Correction can work at the end of reproof or at the end of rebuke depending on our choice of when to respond. If the man walking towards the cliff edge had responded to the initial cries of reproof he would have avoided the painful rebuke of being knocked to the ground and would have received correction of his course long before the edge of the cliff.

Without fail every chastisement from the Father involves correction. Our accountability is to respond swiftly and look for the correction in the lessons. If we don't open our eyes to the lesson in the correction we are doomed to repeat the course. Consider again the analogy of the man who was just tackled at the edge of the cliff. What would be his end if he did not receive a correction to his course? The answer, of course, is that he would need to be tackled again and again until he corrected his course. And believe this for a fact – if the Father has to knock you down a hundred times to keep you from going to disaster, He will do so faithfully.

This can become a miserable cycle but He would rather have a son or daughter covered in dust and bruised than suffer the complete loss of His child forever. It is even recorded in the scriptures that He takes some of His children home early to save them from eternal loss.

Our Part In Chastisement

Our part in the processes of chastisement is first to understand and admit to our need for chastisement. Chastisement is a natural part of growing up in God's house. Secondly we must be willing to submit to His nurturing process in humility and with childlike trust in our heavenly Father's intentions. When we do these things we are truly His children and eventually gain the fullness of everything He made available to us through the work of salvation.

As we grow older in this school of discipline we gradually learn to respond quickly to chastisements. This is expected. It is similar to a natural child requiring less critical levels of chastisement as the child approaches young adulthood.

In the church where I serve I am part of a ministry team comprised of pastors, elders, deacons and ministry leaders of a variety of ages and maturity levels. Within this group the response level to personal chastisement varies dramatically. Those who are less exercised in the process of chastisement often take weeks, months, or years to learn the lessons intended in the chastisement. The more mature members of this team respond much quicker and with greater joy and humility. In particular one of our elders is the quickest to respond.

Luke was blessed from birth with a very bold and fearless personality. Unfortunately, from time to time, and he would be the first to admit, this tendency to boldness causes unintended offenses to other people. As senior pastor, one of my duties is to preserve the peace in the church. As part of this labor I do my best to help resolve any situation where one church member has offended another. Over the years, and on every occasion, as I approached Luke about any offense he might have caused, he not only responded in humility but always dropped everything he was doing and made things right between himself and the one he offended. He would literally jump up at the moment the reproof came and go to the offended party's home to ask for forgiveness, no matter the time of day or the pressures of his own schedule. On more than a few occasions, he even went as far as to wake the person up in the middle of the night to ask forgiveness and once traveled across the United States to spend only a few hours repenting to someone he had offended. This man fulfills his part in the process of God's chastisements as a mature child of God. The fruit in his own life is a man who is continually growing in the knowledge of God, going from glory to glory, and obtaining the fullness of life the Father intended for him. In spite of his often-grating personality, he flows in a greater wisdom and depth of understanding than I have witnessed in many men, and is a joy to work with him.

Luke has learned that responding obediently and faithfully to chastisement means greater life and peace. He has grown to understand the need for chastisement, and has learned to trust his heavenly Father's good intentions in it. As a grown child of God he now takes comfort in this powerful tool of change that his heavenly Father uses to preserve him today and prepare him to prosper tomorrow.

***

Our Part In His School

We've explored quite a bit about life with our Father in His school. The key to benefiting from our Father's school goes back to the promise revealed in the first chapter of Peter; To experience everything He has made available to us we must come to know Him.

Consider again a little baby learning to walk. During the process the parent continuously calls out to the child with words of encouragement and instruction. When a step is taken the parent encourages and cheers. When the child stumbles the parent offers instruction on the correct way to walk. When the child falls the parent speaks words of comfort. Though this continual verbal communication the child learns how things are done, and, begins to learn about the heart of the parent.

This is how we learn of Him in His school. When we begin, He calls to us by His Word (the holy scriptures of the Bible) preached by His servants. These words inspire us to get up and try. They give us faith to take that first step. When we stumble, His Word is there to offer us correction and to show us how it is done. When we fall, His Word is there again to pick us up and comfort us.

Our part in this is to study. Studying is a natural part of any school. His school is not any different. His studies are better in fact because they are living studies.

So how do we study? Here's a good example: Let's say you are facing great tribulation over finances. Distress is all around you. Fear is raging in your heart. You do not know where to turn! How do you learn in this scenario? You begin by running to His Word, the Bible. You search, dig and digest every scripture you can find concerning money, wealth, riches, stewardship etc. This is true studying. In this pressure situation you are sure to learn well. After you have found everything noted on the subject of your pain you meditate on it, memorizing it and locking it deep in your hearts. You pray – talking sincerely to your Father about the situation. And you listen. You listen to the Holy Ghost, the teacher, and to experienced elder brothers and sisters in the church who can counsel you on exactly what the Word from the Bible means and how to use it. Then, you use what you have learned. You put it into practice. You start moving. As you respond by faith (with action) using what you've learned in your daily life, searching Him out in His Word, and talking to Him about it in prayer, the indwelling teacher (the Holy Spirit) guides you into the truth and teaches you about our Father. The result of your studying and using His Word is the knowing of His thoughts concerning finances. Glory! Do you see how simple that is? By running to Him in His Word during a tribulation, we have not only learned how to succeed financially, but we have also learned a small part of our Father's character.

I am told that I am very much like my earthly mother and father. This is to be expected. (And in the case of my parents, it is an honor to me.) Why? - Because their words are in me. I took on a portion of their nature after twenty years in their home under their instruction. This happened very naturally as they instructed me in life while I was growing. I learned what was in their hearts concerning relationships, work, fair play, giving, etc. Their words and ways worked inside my heart until I became as they are. I benefited from everything they had to offer me because I came to the full knowledge of their life.

As God's children we gain the benefits of the life He gave us by coming to know Him as we live with Him through the joys and the challenges that come our way. Through this process He lives with us. This is a pleasure to Him and life to us.

Finally, our part in this is not to go out and suck up general knowledge from every book ever written. Knowledge can become like a drug to you. That is a very bad habit that usually just puffs us up with pride. Your Father will lead you into each of the lessons that He desires you to learn. You don't need to go looking for them. Just pay attention to the challenge of today. There is enough to learn about in what you are going through today. Take no thought for tomorrow. It will come, and He will be there before you arrive.

PART THREE

RUN-AWAYS

One day you will fall. You will come face to face with your darkness. You will turn your back on your Father. You might even walk away. One day you will need to come home to Him. On that day, He will be waiting with open arms.

Chapter 12

Unacceptable Fear

My son let out a scream that curdled my blood. It was 9:30 pm and, until that moment, dead silent in our house. My wife and I leapt to our feet from the living room couch, stumbled and clawed our way frantically up the stairs to rescue our four-year-old boy from whatever beast was devouring him in his bedroom. Hearts pounding we raced through the door, flicked the light on and landed at his bedside all in one motion. "What's wrong? What's wrong?" we gasped breathlessly in stereo. Slowly two little white knuckled hands slipped out over the top of the covers followed by two little eyes as wide as golf balls. A muffled whispering sound came from beneath the covers, "Mmmmonnsttterrrrssss!" Reaching gently under the covers I lifted my boy out of the bed, gave him a big hug and passed him to Mommy.

"Why are you so frightened son?" I asked softly. "Daddy, the night light went out and I saw monsters in my closet and under my bed," he moaned. Together we walked across the room, much to his objection and, after Mommy threw open the closet and hit the light, we looked around inside the closet. "Nope. No monsters in there," I declared. He was happy, but cast a glance of concern to the underworld of the bed. Crossing the room with newfound courage we all got down on our bellies and searched the regions of darkness under his bed. "Nothing! We are safe!" I shouted in victory. A big smile lit up his face. I replaced the nightlight bulb. My wife read him a story and he drifted off to sleep. All was well again in his heart.

Most little children experience the fear of darkness. A child's natural reaction to a dark bedroom is to halt at the threshold and withdraw to cry out for Mom or Dad to come get the lights on. Of course, there is nothing to fear in that dark room. The room is basically the same in the darkness as it is with the light on. But the darkness becomes a vast world of unknown evil to a child's mind. What is it that causes a three year old to quit at the threshold of a dark room? The answer is simply that the child lacks the understanding that the room is the same in the dark as in the light.

Unwarranted fear is the direct result of a lack of understanding. My son had no reason to fear monsters under his bed. But at that age there is a youthful ignorance of the facts. In place of understanding, my child was forced to rely on his imagination to analyze the situation. In the face of darkness and lacking understanding, his imagination filled the room with all sorts of terrible monsters, bandits, and ghosts waiting to jump out from hidden places. These imagined dangers grew more powerful in his mind the more he thought on them. Finally the fear reached panic level and he cried out.

When we heard the blood curdling screams of our son, we raced to his aid expecting to find him in the midst of some terrible predicament. With the child clutching to Mom's leg trembling on his way to search out the closet with us, he blubbered out a string of rambling stories about seeing something move in the dark and hearing some strange noises. As we crossed the room to his closet, Mom shook her head wearing a gentle smile and said, "Oh, honey. There is nothing in there, see." And, with the flick of the light switch, our son bounced into the brightly lit closet, grabbed up a stuffed animal and headed off to search under the bed. It's amazing what a bit of light can do to a lot of darkness.

During childhood this level of fear is acceptable. But what would we think of someone who is still afraid of the dark as an adult? Children who run from darkness and the unknown are

The Better Life of Knowing God

judged as cute or silly. An adult who is fearful of entering a dark room has a serious problem.

When we are growing up in our heavenly Father's house, it is understandable that we would draw back from the unknown and quit at the threshold of certain doors. Maturing progressively away from certain of life's fears is a natural process. To remain in an unwarranted fear too long, however, spells disaster to our future growth and cuts us off from really getting to know our Father.

My children grew out of their fear of the dark by the gentle and persistent encouragements of my wife and I. Initially we went through the process of walking them hand-in-hand through a dark room. After a season of this, we encouraged them to go-it-alone while we stood at the door. From there they went in while we stood at the end of the hall. At every stage of growth each of our children haltingly and cautiously inched into the dark room. This was still cute and expected. Finally, at a certain age, we put on the pressure by encouraging each child to face the darkness alone. During this season of growth our children were faced with the reality that they were either going to do it alone or not go at all. Not going at all meant that they would be forced to go without a toy they wanted to play with that was stored in that dark, dark room. It always worked. The desire for the toy overcame the fear of darkness. At first they would make a mad leaping dash for the light switch, (in our old house they were very high and usually behind the door) then, racing across the room, they would swoop up the toy and fly back down the steps in one blinding motion. After repeating this course several dozen times, each of our children learned that there was never really anything to fear. They learned the truth about dark rooms. A light came on in their understanding and the truth set them free.

When We Run and Hide

What if my children never overcame the fear of darkness? There would of course be a very sad loss of opportunity. They would have never been able to get to their toys alone. They would never be able to sleep alone. My wife and I would have been run ragged by the age of thirty escorting them to and from their toy chests every evening. This is much like what occurs in the life of a believer when he or she does not grow out of simple fears.

When we draw back or run and hide from the challenges and difficulties of our new life in the kingdom of our Father, we needlessly doom ourselves to a life of less, or to a life where others must endlessly escort us.

Scripture teaches us that we learn, *"line upon line and precept upon precept."* Our learning process is much like the construction of a brick building. Each higher course of bricks is laid upon, and depends on, the course laid previously beneath it. If a brick mason tries to lay a third course of bricks before laying the second course, he will fail. When we fail to learn a certain lesson or fail to grow out of a certain youthful fear in our new life in Christ, we are stuck. Or, as often occurs, we lay upper courses of experience on top of incomplete lower courses. By running from any one of the pre-arranged challenges that our heavenly Father sends our way, we are leaving out important parts of our spiritual education about who He is and how He works. These missing building blocks inevitably show up in the future when the cracks in our faith and missing pieces of our knowledge of Him begin to rob us of our peace and joy. Eventually this failure to learn causes us to lock-up at a certain growth stage until we learn what we missed. In our earthly schools this is known as being held back to repeat a grade.

Being held back often comes as a direct result of failing to do assignments and/or failing tests. In school, homework trains us day by day and tests are used through the school year to prove what we have learned. If we pass a certain number of tests on any particular subject we are given the opportunity to move on to the next level. If we fail the tests we are held back from the opportunity to move on. Being held back is always traumatic but not cruel. A good, caring teacher knows that a student who fails to learn basic math in first grade will only suffer worse in second grade math.

In our spiritual lives we are always in a process of learning and testing. Our heavenly Father carefully arranges a life full of homework for each believer. Each opportunity, no matter the size or shape, is divinely supervised and tailored to each of us individually. As a good parent, God works with us patiently teaching us to grow out of the fear of life's darkness. He loves us enough to insist that we learn each lower lesson before giving us the opportunity to move on to greater lessons and opportunities. Graduating us too soon would only spell future disaster for us.

As mentioned at the conclusion of the last chapter, our part in His school is to apply ourselves diligently to study as we pass through each learning opportunity. When we draw back in fear, anger, or frustration for an extended period of time it is the equivalent of running and hiding. This is not acceptable. Fear, frustration, and anger are not faith. When we draw back this way we are making a statement with our actions saying that we do not believe in Him enough to protect us, teach us, deliver us from disaster, or provide for us. This rejection of our Father's love is a personal offense to God. Failing a test is not a problem but running and hiding from a test is a problem.

Running Backwards

All believers who run from life's challenges run in the same direction - backwards. Historically, after each great spiritual move of God around the world, we witness a mass exodus of new-believers running back to former familiar lifestyles. Moses witnessed the same phenomena when he was leading the nation of Israel out of slavery from Egypt.

After four hundred years of crying out to God for deliverance from captivity, the Israelites found themselves in the desert outside of Egypt, free at last. They had just witnessed the incredible miracles of the plagues that led up to their newfound freedom. They departed from Egypt carrying a fortune in precious metals and supplies given to them by their former oppressors. They were finally able to worship and live as they liked. The Lord had done a mighty thing in their lives, including leading them with a supernatural pillar of fire that burned day and night. But in spite of all these wonders and answers to prayers, they were ready to run back to their old lives when the first sign of difficulty arose.

As these children of God traveled from Egypt they came to the banks of the Red Sea led by the amazing pillar of fire. But from the distance came a rumbling of chariot wheels. Pharaoh, the king of Egypt, was after them with vengeance in his heart. Seeing this army approaching like a mighty dust storm caused a wave of panic through God's people camped along the sea. Bone chilling fear quickly replaced the spirit of euphoria that was present up until that moment. In desperation, they rushed to Moses.

You would think that these people who had witnessed so many miracles of deliverance should be full of faith and fearlessness. In reality the opposite was true. As they approached Moses they cried as one voice, "We would be better off in Egypt! You should have left us there! We would rather die there in slavery than face this!" They were ready to go back into terrible bondage and die slowly rather than face this one difficulty. As crazy as it sounds, they were prepared to run and hide in the familiar pain of slavery rather than stand and face this present challenge with faith in their God.

Later in their journey across the desert they repeated their cry to return to Egypt. On this second occasion, they had just heard the report of their own spies who were sent into the Promised Land to scout it out before they entered. Two of the returning spies told wondrous tales of a land flowing with milk and honey and showed samples of the fruit of the land. Other spies, however, reported on how strong and terrible the people of the lands were, and how impossible it would be to face and overcome them.

Upon hearing the reports, the people cried out again to return to Egypt rather than face the challenge of the giants of the Promised Land. There they were on the verge of walking into a living prophecy of abundance. But paralyzed with fear they turned back into the harsh desert and missed this opportunity.

Returning to what is behind and familiar during trials and testing is tempting. It always seems easier to go back to what is known than to press on into the unknown. Believers faced with the lessons and trials of life have a simple choice: go forward in childlike faith or turn back to what is familiar. By turning back we fall just short of gaining the fullness of what lies on the other side of the challenge. We miss the chance to see more of Him and learn more about His love for us. Those who run from the Father's lessons walk in circles until they decide to return to the lesson. But take heart. When you return He will still be there to walk you through it.

Turning back is not an option. The scriptures state that it would be better for us never to have been born than to start our journey in Jesus and turn back. In the gospel of Luke chapter 9, verse 62, Jesus stated,

> *"Anyone who puts a hand to the plow and then looks back is not fit for the Kingdom of God."* (NLT)

When we make a habit of running back to, and hiding in, what is familiar, comfortable, and safe we cause an offense to our heavenly Father's heart. It is sad to witness a child of God run back to former shallow lifestyles or into lifeless religious traditions rather than moving forward in childlike faith trusting Him to protect, teach, and make provision.

This was the sin of the Israelites who constantly murmured against God while traveling out of bondage from Egypt to freedom. In spite of all the miraculous provision the Lord made for them in their journey, they continued to complain and plot to return to Egypt. In the end their attitude toward the challenges they faced caused God to refuse them entrance into the Promised Land.

In the early days of their journey, the Lord responded to their murmurings by comforting them and giving them what they cried for. But as time passed, and they continued to murmur in the face of repeated answers from God, He changed His response to curses and plagues. In the desert the Father longed for His chosen people to trust Him and learn. Just as parents labor faithfully in patience to teach their young children not to fear the dark, so did He with those who feared hunger, thirst, and destruction in that wilderness journey. But they refused to believe in Him.

The Israelites lived under the Old Testament of the Law. Fortunately, for us today, we live under the New Testament of grace. Because of the sacrifice of Jesus, God no longer sends down curses and plagues when His people miss the mark. But the wages for running back still take a heavy toll on our lives by cutting us off from the fullness of everything He is. When we turn back and refuse to face the lessons of our life, we end up in the land of confusion leading to bitterness, deeper sin and useless pursuits of the flesh. Eventually we become entangled again in the web of death and destruction that we were originally delivered from at the point of our salvation. Most frustrating of all is the reality that we no longer fit in those former ways. When we come to salvation we are changed forever. All the rules are changed. No matter how we try, the old ways never again bring us comfort. When we enter this new life our old man is buried by the death and burial of Jesus. The new man simply will not fit into the old life. It's like trying to put a square peg into a round hole. We end up more frustrated than ever.

Our heavenly Father knows all of our fears. In His goodness He has prepared a life full of challenges for us. In His gentleness He never brings us to a challenge we cannot face. In His patience He never expects us to enter the dark rooms that come our way on the first try. Our part is to trust Him like a child and stay with Him to learn. When we do this, He has opportunity to teach us to not fear and opportunity to fellowship with us in our maturing processes.

Hide and Blame

As a pastor, my main goal is to keep the Lord's sheep on a path of growth towards maturity. Part of that task involves finding sheep that have strayed from the path of life and gone into hiding. This may seem a simple task until you consider that in most cases those who go into hiding still attend church services regularly and even continue in church ministry work while their soul and spirit are somewhere else. But inevitably the blame-game will begin.

In recalling the example of the Israelites in the wilderness, we notice that they not only murmured and wished to return to Egypt, but also constantly placed all the blame on Moses. Why not blame God? Why did they blame Moses? The answer is simple. If we use God for an excuse to turn back we are really admitting that we ourselves are wrong because most Christians know enough about God to know that He is never wrong.

If we cannot blame God, and would never blame ourselves, we must then of course place the blame on other people. This is what the Israelites did to Moses. Rather than blame God, they blamed Moses for leading them out into the desert. Literally they were calling Moses a fraud. This was the only way they could feel justified in turning back and still live with themselves.

The problem with blaming Moses was that God took it personally. Since God Himself had sent Moses, Moses represented God. Consequently when they blamed Moses, they were actually, in God's eyes, blaming Him. This is the downfall of many who descend to the point of laying blame on others for their desire to run. By blaming others, we willfully step out of the realm of humility and separate ourselves from the grace (divine help) of God. God opposes the proud.

> *Yea, all of you be subject one to another, and be clothed with humility: for God resisteth the proud, and giveth grace to the humble.*
> 1 Peter 5:5b (KJV)

Convincing yourself that you are a victim of the actions or choices of other people only hastens your descent into bitterness, which is the next step of a downward spiral.

Many people go into hiding and live out their entire lives serving in churches with no one noticing. The sad reality is that these folks fit perfectly into structured church service where they are not called on to make Spirit-led decisions on their own. For this reason they are often hard to spot. They can work out their lives having every appearance of a faithful servant, when in reality they are hiding in the comfort of what is familiar. They are always there, but never quite enter into the fullness of life the way others do. They are hidden well, and suffer alone. They use their talents to serve, but never press on into the next realm. When a situation arises that is beyond their own abilities or their understanding, they draw back or remain silent. And sadly, if they do not change their course, they never go on to grow in their knowledge of the Father.

Back to the Flesh

The more obvious place that we hide from God is in the land of our old ways - the flesh. When we run backwards, we inevitably end up where we came from originally. If we were heavily involved in immorality before our conversion, we will probably end up hiding in the same sin to some degree when we run from the challenges of our new life. The familiar things that once gave us comfort and sensual happiness are all we know to return to. Some hide in their careers, their hobbies, entertainment, alcohol, pursuits of earthly wealth, etc. When it comes to hiding, we can be very creative and diverse. The list of hiding places is endless, but the result is always the same: no rest, no peace, no contentment, no growth, and no fullness. We miss it all when we hide in our flesh. The flesh is a nasty place to live. It eats up everything good like a swarm of locusts. Going back there always makes matters worse.

And when people escape from the wickedness of the world by knowing our Lord and Savior Jesus Christ and then get

tangled up and enslaved by sin again, they are worse off than before.
2 Peter 2:20 (NLT)

    The Lord takes no delight when we run away or turn back. But truly it is our choice. He gives us that great freedom to decide. And in His great mercy He also gives us the way back home. When we run we rob ourselves of the better life of knowing God and of course we rob Him of our presence, which is the greatest tragedy of all.

    If you are crippled in fear, lost in mediocrity or have run from your Father - take hope! You can come home to a better life.

Chapter 13

Free to Choose or Refuse

One day you will fall. You will come face to face with your darkness. You will turn your back on your Father. You might even walk away. One day you will need to come home to Him. On that day, He will be waiting with open arms.

Restoration is a wonderful thing. Years ago a young man who abandoned God and left our church to chase his own desires, returned. He came to me beaten and broken asking to be restored to membership. I am sure he expected a rebuke or a long sermon from me, but the only thing I had in my heart was great joy. I told him I would meet with the elders immediately to convey his request. At that elder's meeting there was no discussion of any pre-restoration penalty payment. In fact, the only thing we discussed was planning a big church picnic to celebrate his return.

A week later the entire church met on a local farm, decorated the trees and driveway with welcome home signs and balloons, and we all received him back into full fellowship in accordance with the Spirit of our Father. Today he is married to a woman of God. And though he still suffers in certain ways as a result of the death he fell into as a runaway, every day brings greater restoration, and all things in his life are being made to work for the good. This is our Father's great mercy to His runaways.

True sons and daughters are always free to choose the life and fellowship of their Father or reject it. The ultimate joy of the Father comes when we freely choose to be with Him because we really deeply love Him, not for what He can give us or do for us, but because we just want to be with Him.

In the parable of the prodigal son (Luke, Chapter 15) Jesus taught us how the Father responds when we freely choose Him, even after refusing Him. Being the proverbial prodigal son myself, this story always brings tears to my eyes.

***

Saul was just moving the last of his father's sheep through the gate when he heard the servant Zelinus calling, "*MASTER SAUL! MASTER SAUL, HAVE YOU HEARD?*"

"Zelinus, why are you running? What has happened? Is my father all right?" asked Saul.

"Yes Master. He is fine," replied Zelinus panting for air.

"Sit down and catch your breath," instructed Saul as Zelinus collapsed against the gate.

"Now, what is it? What should I have heard?" asked Saul.

"It's your younger brother," Zelinus began.

Saul interrupted with concern, "Elias? What has happened to him? Is he hurt?"

"No Master, he is fine," replied Zelinus.

"Well then, what is it?" demanded Saul.

"I just came from your father's house. He is dividing up the inheritance," reported Zelinus.

Saul was shocked. "*WHAT? WHY?*" he cried.

"It is Elias. He went to your father this morning and asked for his share. The servants are tallying it up now. I heard that he plans to leave in the morning!" said Zelinus.

"How can this be? What is he thinking? Why would he wish to leave?" asked Saul turning to pull the gate shut.

"I don't know, Master. But he looked determined to go," replied Zelinus.

"But what has my father said? Has he tried to stop him?" asked Saul.

"I overheard him telling another of the servants that all of his sons are free to do as they wish," replied Zelinus, "Master, where are you going?" he asked as Saul ran for the house.

"I must find Elias. I'm going to knock some sense into him. He is acting like a fool," grunted Saul.

***

"ELIAS! ELIAS, COME OUT HERE!" Saul yelled from the courtyard in front of the house.

"Saul? What is it? Why are you shouting?" asked Elias cautiously emerging from the front door.

"Elias, one of our servants just told me that you are planning to take your inheritance and leave. Is that true?" demanded Saul.

"Yes, it is true," Elias declared proudly.

"*WHAT HAS GOTTEN INTO YOU? ARE YOU CRAZY? FATHER HAS BEEN SO GOOD TO YOU! HOW CAN YOU LEAVE HIM NOW?*" demanded Saul menacingly.

"Brother, I just want to leave and I'm going!" declared Elias.

"Going where? Where are you going?" continued Saul.

"I'm not sure yet. I heard there is a lot going on in the land to the east. I'm going to check it out," said Elias moving back into the house.

"EAST! There is nothing but wickedness in the land to the east! Why would you want to go there?" Saul asked following Elias into the foyer.

Elias hesitated for a moment peering around the corner to the front room to see if father was listening. He whispered, "I heard there are parties that go on day and night over there, and women..."

"STOP!" cried Saul in outrage, "I don't want to hear anymore! *JUST GO!*" Saul shoved Elias aside as he passed by.

"But Saul, I..." tried Elias.

Saul continued through the doorway, and yelled back, "Just go, Elias. Go on, go."

***

Elias found his father in his chair holding a heavy leather purse. "Father, I am ready to go. May I have my share now?" asked Elias.

"Yes Elias. Here it is," replied his father quietly.

Elias gently took the bag from his aged father's fingers. "Father. I am sorry. I do not mean to hurt you," he said.

"I will miss you my son," his father said as he grasped Elias's hand.

"Father..." started Elias.

His father interrupted, "Go now Elias. You are free."

Elias slipped out the back door into the evening shades.

***

Elias hit town just in time for the nightly festivities. He popped into the first hotel on the street and introduced himself to the owner, "Hello, my name is Elias."

"Elias! Good to meet you. How can I help you?" replied the owner.

"I want the biggest and best room in your hotel and I've got money to pay for it," boasted Elias.

"Very well sir. Right this way. My name is Balak. Anything you need, just call on me," chirped Balak with glee.

Balak had the appearance of a grubby kitchen cook. But Elias didn't much notice.

"Any parties going on around town Mr. Balak?" inquired Elias.

"*PARTIES!* You want parties? We got parties! You came to the right place! Just leave everything to me. I'll get a few of my friends together and we'll bust the walls off the city tonight! How much money do you have anyhow?" asked Balak leaning closer to Elias.

"I got plenty. I just got my inheritance," reported Elias.

"OH MAN! LET'S GET TO IT! I really like you. What did you say your name was? Elibu?" asked a now giddy Balak.

"Elias. My name is Elias," Elias corrected a bit annoyed.

"Oh yeah. Elias. Well Elias, I know these two women who..." Balak rambled on as the two men settled in front of the fireplace with a bottle of strong wine.

***

Elias rolled over slightly on his sleeping mat at the sound of men in armor clamoring down the hallway outside his room. "Who dares disturb my sleep?" he barked with a raspy voice. "Can't a man get any sleep here?" he cried.

Just then the door burst open and two burly constables, a captain and his aide, stepped into the room with Mr. Balak in tow. "There he is officer. Get him out of here," Balak demanded, "He is two months past due on his room rent. He is a bum," declared the once friendly Balak.

Elias rolled back onto his face and groaning said, "Go away! Can't you see I'm resting?"

"Hey you! Get up! Mr. Balak wants you out. Get up!" demanded the captain. "Mr. Balak, what is his name?" demanded the captain's aide.

"His name? I don't know. I think it is Elibu or Elobi or something like that. Just get him out of here. He has been begging from my other guests and making a nuisance of himself. He has been drunk for the last three months. He is penniless! He's no friend of mine. I just want rid of him," demanded Balak.

"Very well Mr. Balak," agreed the captain as he and his aide commenced dragging Elias out by his feet.

"What... what, who... is... it... wha... what... do you want? Can't you see I'm sleeping?" asked a bloodshot-eyed Elias.

"It's the police. It's the middle of the afternoon! Get up. You need to get out of here," demanded the captain.

"But why? Hey Balak, tell them who I am," Elias whined.

"Get lost, jerk! You haven't paid me in weeks. I need this room," said Balak as he threw Elias' sandals out the window.

"But what about all the good times we had? You said that I could count on you," Elias said as the constables dropped him most ungraciously into the lobby.

"Officers, if you do not get him out of here, I am going to do it myself," warned Balak.

"Okay, okay. I'm going," relented Elias.

"Good riddance," replied Balak throwing the last of Elias' meager belongings out the door behind him.

Elias stumbled his way two blocks before bumping headlong into another constable.

"Sir, do you have a job or a place to stay?" asked the constable.

"No my good friend, I don't," replied Elias as graciously as he could while still a bit drunk from the previous night's reveling.

"Well you better find a place," demanded the constable, "We don't allow bums in this town."

"But where can I go?" asked Elias, "I have no more money and no friends, and there are no jobs because of the drought. What can I do?"

"That is your problem buddy," replied the constable, then looking on Elias with a bit of pity he declared, "I shouldn't, but I'll give you a day to find a place or move on."

"Thank you officer," Elias said as he stumbled by.

"And take a bath," the officer yelled, "You smell like a wine barrel."

Elias paused to smell his tunic. "Yes sir," he replied.

***

The officer's grace period was long over by three days. Elias was desperate. It was time to start begging. "Hello, my name is Elias. I'm looking for work," he asked humbly as he walked through a farmer's gate.

"Yeah, you and everyone else in this region," replied the grizzled old farmer, "Get lost."

"But sir, I am skilled at farming. My father owned many fields and livestock," Elias noted with bended knee.

"Big deal, I can't afford another employee," replied the farmer with growing annoyance.

"But I'll work for nothing. Just give me a place to sleep and some scraps to eat," offered Elias in tears.

"Okay, okay. Stop it! If you wish, you can work with the pigs and eat their slop. Get a bucket and go out to feed them. You can sleep in the barn with them. That's all I can do for you," declared the farmer as he walked away in obvious disgust.

"Thank you, sir," replied Elias quietly.

The farmer threw his hand into the air in contempt and continued on his way.

Elias awoke to swine shrieking all around him. "What am I doing here in this land? Oh father...father...what have I done?" Elias wept, "Why did I ever leave you? Even the very least of your servants has more than enough to eat. I wish I could go home. Yes, that is what I will do. I will go back to my father. I will fall at his feet and beg for just a small job as one of his servants. At least I will have something to eat. But what will he say? How can I go back after what I have done? I have shamed him. I walked out on him and spit on his love for me. I have sinned a thousand sins and used up everything he gave me. But I must go back. *I WILL GO BACK! FATHER! I'M COMING HOME!"*

Elias leapt over the rails of the pigpen, threw off his filthy coat, and raced down the road toward his father's country.

***

"*MASTER! MASTER!*" called Zelinus.

"Yes Zelinus, what is it?" asked the father.

"*LOOK! THERE IN THE DISTANCE!*" Zelinus said with excitement.

"Who is it Zelinus? I can't quite make him out. It looks a little like... my... *MY SON! ELIAS MY SON HAS COME HOME!*" the father cried.

"Master! Wait for me!" laughed Zelinus trying to keep up.

"Hurry, Zelinus. It is my son!" yelled the father as he threw off his beautiful robes to run faster.

Elias' heart raced as he saw his dad running at him. "Is he angry? Will he fall upon me with blows of wrath?" he wondered. As his father approached he blurted, "Father, I have sinned and am not worthy to be called your son anymore. I have..." But the force of his father's hugs cut him off.

"ZELINUS!" cried his father, "Run and get the best robe from my closet and put it on my son!"

"But Father, I have sinned and..." Elias started.

"And Zelinus, get the family ring from my chest and put it on his hand," instructed the father.

"But Father, I left you and..." Elias started again.

"And Zelinus, get a pair of shoes for his feet," instructed the father with a mighty laugh.

"Oh Father. I am not worthy, I..." Elias tried again.

"And Zelinus, go to the barn, get the prize calf that we have been saving! Prepare it for cooking," shouted his father to Zelinus who was already running back to the house.

"But Father I lost everything. How can I ever..." Elias started but was cut off again.

"And Zelinus, one more thing, get the house ready for a party! *TELL EVERYONE THAT MY SON HAS COME HOME! HE WAS LOST BUT NOW HE IS WITH ME! IT IS TIME TO CELEBRATE!*" shouted the father, "Elias, my son, come to the house and we will celebrate!" he said wrapping his arm around his son.

"But Father," Elias insisted, "listen to me. I have lost everything you gave me. I have lived with pigs and shamed your name in many places. I am not worthy to..."

"*ELIAS!*" interrupted his Father, "*YOU ARE MY CHILD!* Today I have my son back with me! This is your home. You belong here with me. I love you, Elias. All the riches in my kingdom are not as valuable to me as having you back in my house. Look, here comes Zelinus. He has your robe."

***

Mature Fellowship Demands Freedom of Choice

Freedom is an incredible thing. Once we accept the salvation given us by Jesus we become totally and completely free. In this freedom, we are not only made free from the controlling power of sin and death, but we also become free to choose life, or, to turn from it.

This complete freedom is necessary if we are to fulfill our Father's desire for sincere fellowship that is based on true love. Why? For true love to exist between two parties, each party must be free to refuse that love. If we were not made totally free to choose God's love, or turn it down, our fellowship would be of no value to Him. He can create slaves anytime. He is not interested in fellowshipping with or living with those who do not choose His life willingly.

A good analogy of the need for freedom in a relationship is like a man who desperately wants a son but because of sterility can't reproduce. In his frustration he goes out and kidnaps a grown child. When he brings the child home, he joyfully sets about the process of giving the child everything he needs. But alas, something is wrong. The child does not love the man. In fact, he hates him because of his captivity. And the man has gained no fulfillment because the kidnapped son only obeys and fellowships as a captive slave. There is no real relationship between them at all other than the relationship of a master and a prisoner.

If salvation meant only freedom from sins, it would not be enough. Salvation also means freedom from unwilling slavery of any kind. If we were not free to choose or reject God's life after salvation, we would not be truly free. This is an incredible act of love on the part of our heavenly Father. In spite of the fact that He gave everything to save us, we can still choose to run and hide from Him and avoid His fellowship *EVEN AFTER SALVATION.*

And hear this - if we choose to run and/or hide from Him, He will honor our decision. It will grieve Him just as it would grieve an earthly father but, out of respect for our freedom, He will not stop us. He will do everything He can to convince us not to go. But in the end, He will let us go. He gave us that freedom so that those who willingly choose to live with Him will be doing so in free will. This is true love. This is how He wants to be loved. He wants to be loved just for who He is. Don't you?

When we come to initial salvation we gain great treasure in His life and Kingdom. Everyone loves this part of their relationship to God. At the point of salvation our souls are released from the burdens of guilt and confusion. Everything becomes fresh and new. This is our experience of Jesus the Savior.

The problem usually begins when we meet Jesus the Lord. With great wealth comes great accountability. When the reality of accountability hits home, many respond by drawing back or by taking the money and running. This usually occurs when we grow a little and are asked to take on more work, love other people in greater measure, or give more out of the treasure He gave us. In the freedom that the Savior bought for us, we can choose either way.

> *"Listen! A farmer went out to plant some seeds. As he scattered them across his field, some seeds fell on a footpath, and the birds came and ate them. Other seeds fell on shallow soil with underlying rock. The seeds sprouted quickly because the soil was shallow. But the plants soon wilted under the hot sun, and since they didn't have deep roots, they died. Other seeds fell among thorns that grew up and choked out the tender plants. Still other seeds fell on fertile soil, and they produced a crop that was thirty, sixty, and even a hundred times as much as had been planted! Anyone with ears to hear should listen and understand.*
> "Matthew 13:3b-9 (NLT)

When we choose to mature and face the accountability of His freedom we are blessed with greater opportunity, but when we run, we always run-out of freedom. You may think that running will make your life easier or more enjoyable, but the opposite is true. It only makes you poorer and robs your heavenly Father and His people of your presence.

Even so, God loves the ones who run and waits patiently in that love until they come to their senses and return to His arms. This is the great mercy of our Father. Even when we reject Him in foolishness, He still freely chooses to love us. In this there is great hope for the runaways.

The parable of the prodigal son is truly a great revelation of our freedom, our Father's mercy, and His desire to have us return to fellowship. The prodigal son started with a great inheritance just as we do when we come to our Father's house. He had everything he needed for life and godliness right in his father's home, just as we do in our heavenly Father's home. But the prodigal wanted it all without the accountability that came with being the son of a rich man.

As the rich man's son he was expected to serve in his father's fields: tend livestock, manage servants, etc. He loved the good things of his father's house and farm, but he wanted to do his own thing. At the point of leaving, he only loved his father for what his father could give him.

When he ran he took his inheritance with him and used it in selfishness to gain personal pleasures. He believed that by running from accountability he would be able to enjoy the good things without care for the tough things that came with growing up and serving in his father's life. When he ran he thought he had found freedom.

Many believers fall to this deception. Running never makes our life better or easier. If a challenge, tribulation, or chastisement has come your way, be sure to know that He expects you to face it where you are. Running from people who offend you, running from service to his kingdom, or running from things you do not understand will gain you nothing. In fact, you will end up a hundred times worse, and as the prodigal son discovered, the end of such choices never justify the means and never produce freedom.

All the treasure you can carry out of His kingdom will not keep you from the disaster that befell the prodigal son. Stay where you are and face that tribulation, challenge, or service in His strength. Do not ever believe that you have the option to abandon Him or His family just because you don't like them or you disagree with God's ways. You cannot separate from the people He has made you one with by the sacrifice of His Son Jesus. We are all one in Him. And you cannot be free from Him in a universe where His life governs everything.

If you are already in escape - take heart! You can go back and be re-established in the fullness of His love! Just get up out of that hiding place and go back in humility as the prodigal did. Fall down before those who you abandoned and ask forgiveness. Fall before the Lord and your heavenly Father and ask forgiveness for rejecting His school, His house, His work and His fellowship. Set aside your pride like the Prodigal Son did. In that place His grace will help you, His mercy will restore you, and you will once again pick up your journey into knowing your Father.

If you are too proud to do these things, you have not yet reached the bottom of your pigpen. You will. *The backslider in heart will have his fill of his own ways* (Proverbs 14:14a NAS) Everyone who runs reaches the bottom. When you get there, remember His goodness and mercy, and go back. Your royal robe, ring, and sandals await you there in the hands of your heavenly Father.

This is the freedom our Father gave us through salvation. Before salvation, we are slaves to the old nature and cannot even choose right over wrong. After salvation, we gain the ability to choose. But salvation does not force us to continue in His life, be part of His local church, or serve Him in His works.

We are free to make those choices every day. We are free to love Him or reject Him on a daily, moment-to-moment basis. His great desire is that we freely choose to love Him. All of His labors through history have been purposed to convince us that he is worthy of that love. In the face of that love, we can all cry out with the Psalmist:

> *When I consider thy heavens, the work of thy fingers, the moon and the stars, which thou hast ordained; what is man, that thou art mindful of him? and the son of man, that thou visitest him? For thou hast made him a little lower than the angels, and hast crowned him with glory and honour. Thou madest him to have dominion over the works of thy hands; thou has put all things under his feet: All sheep and oxen, yea, and the beasts of the field; the fowl of the air, and the fish of the sea, and whatsoever passeth through the paths of the seas. O LORD our Lord, how excellent is they name in all the earth!*
> Psalm 8:3-9 (KJV)

PART FOUR

WITH HIM IN HIS HOUSE

What is your mansion like? What will it be filled with? Well - that is the exciting part of your life in Him - you get to fill it by choosing to love Him today and every day. By becoming all He has destined you to be.

Chapter 14

A Place for You

OK. Strap on your thinking cap with me. This chapter may challenge your way of seeing life as it is now and how you view your eternity.

When I was a young Christian I dreamt often of my ideal heavenly mansion. I pictured it as a massive glass home filled inside and out with plush greenery, beautiful courtyards, comfy leather furniture, a fine dining hall and all of my life's rewards arranged neatly throughout the home. Hmmm...

When did eternity begin? Big news - it has always been, it is now, and it always will be. Eternity was happening long before you were born. It's happening now. When do you get to sit in God's eternal throne next to the Father with Jesus? Bigger news - you are already there. When will your special place be ready for you to move in? Great news - it has been ready and waiting for 2,000+ years. When do you get to move into your heavenly mansion? Best news of all – NOW! Skeptical? Read these quotes from God's Word:

> *God, being rich in mercy, because of His great love with which he loved us, even when we were dead in our transgressions, made us alive together with Christ (by grace you have been saved), and <u>raised us up with Him, and seated us with Him in the heavenly places</u>, in Christ Jesus...*
> Ephesians 2:4-6 (NAS)

> *In my Father's house are many mansions: if it were not so, I would have told you. <u>I go to prepare a place for you</u>.*

John 14:2 (KJV)

If you are challenged to believe this possible, you are not alone. The disciples also had trouble with this truth. Let's visit them after the Last Supper. (Based on the Gospel of John, Chapters 13 & 14)

***

Supper was finished when Jesus spoke to the disciples, "I will not be here with you much longer and you can't come with me right now. But don't get discouraged because I am going to my Father's house to prepare a special place for you, and when it is ready I will come for you."

***

Leaving their supper, the disciples crossed the Kidron ravine towards a grove of olive trees in the distance. Peter, walking with John, spoke in a soft whisper, "He washed our feet. I can't believe that He made us let Him wash our feet. And Judas," Peter's voice fell, "He said Judas would betray Him. I cannot believe he will betray our master."

"Yes, I was shocked," responded John. "Peter why did the master say he was leaving? I thought we were going to start His kingdom here in the city. Where is He going and why can't we go with Him!"

"I don't know John," replied Peter. "I tried to tell Him that I would never ever leave Him and even go to war for Him but all He told me was that I would deny Him three times."

"I'm sorry Peter," comforted John. "There must be some explanation for all this. I'm sure He will help us understand.

Peter took several quiet steps then stopped with a long gaze towards the Lord walking ahead. "He said He was going somewhere to get our special places ready," Peter mused with wonder in his voice. "I just don't understand."

Coming up from behind, Andrew overheard Peter's words. "I don't understand either. We gave up everything to follow the master. Why is He leaving us now? Where will we go? Where is this land He is going to? Why can't he build a place for all of us right here? "Andrew asked.

Peter resumed the journey while answering, "This has been a very long evening. Perhaps tomorrow we will understand His words. Come let's catch up with the master before He goes into the olive groves alone without our protection."

***

Your place is ready - now!

At the Last Supper, Jesus gave His final words of instruction and encouragement to the disciples in preparation for His departure to the Cross. Peter and the other disciples were in shock. Jesus had just dropped a bombshell. After all they had been through with Him and everything they witnessed, they were probably convinced that Jesus was about to take over the world. Instead they are told He is leaving. Picking up on their fears, He comforted them with the promise that He was leaving in order to get their place prepared.

At that time, the disciples had no understanding of the need for Jesus to die. They were still seeing His presence on the earth as the way to set up the kingdom of God right there in Jerusalem. They had no eyes to see that the purpose of Jesus' coming was to bring many sons to the Father by reconciling the world through the sacrifice of His life. When He told them that He was leaving, they could only see personal loss. His response was to lift their minds and hearts into the eternal purposes of

God the Father. He spoke to them about a special place in His Father's house.

Jesus was going away to make a place ready for the Father's new children. By taking His place at the right hand of the Father, He made it possible for us to enter God's house. When He was lifted up to the glory He deserved, he secured our own place in the heavenly realms. And the best of all, when we are born again into His kingdom, we gain entrance into that special place that He prepared. It is not a place that we wait until death to gain entrance to. It is prepared and ready for you to dwell in NOW. All you need to do is move in.

How do we move in? By faith! It is as simple as that. When we believe on Jesus for our new life, we are permitted to enter our Father's house. That faith is what the Father demands. The Father counts our faith in Jesus as righteousness. If we believe, we are permitted to walk right through the front door of His house and right into our place in Him. There are no prior prepayment requirements of good deeds or getting better. Jesus' death on the Cross made the way. Literally, He is the door. All we need to do is reach for the doorknob by faith and walk through believing that the sacrifice of Jesus was enough.

> *Therefore, since we have been justified through faith, we have peace with God through our Lord Jesus Christ, through whom we have gained access by faith into his grace in which we now stand.*
> Romans 5:1-2 (NIV)

To move in by faith, we must first believe there is a place for us. We have already covered that Jesus made that possible. We must also know where His house is located. If we do not know the address, we can't get there. If we don't get there, we will not actually benefit from the good things that His house offers. So, where is His house? And where is our place?

It is closer than you might think.

The House of Our Father
In chapter two, The Tearing of the Veil, we saw the old tabernacle as the imperfect dwelling place of our God. At the death of Jesus, the old imperfect tabernacle was done away with. God's presence moved out of that old tabernacle. He changed residence. He left the confines of that earthly natural building and made His home somewhere else. Where did He go? He went where He always wanted to be. He moved into us. We became his dwelling place.

> *As God hath said, I will dwell in them, and walk in them; and I will be their God and they shall be my people.*
> 2 Corinthians 6:16 (KJV)

> *You are no longer foreigners and aliens, but fellow citizens with God's people and members of God's household, built on the foundation of the apostles and prophets, with Christ Jesus himself as the chief cornerstone. In Him the whole building is joined together and rises to become a holy temple in the Lord. And in Him you are being built together to become a dwelling in which God lives by His Spirit.*
> Ephesians 2:19-22 (NIV)

Our Father's house is made up of all those who believe on Him through the ages. God's house, as revealed on the earth today, is the church. His church is made up of all those who are truly born of His Spirit, those who by faith in His love follow after Him - you and me.

In a particular region or town, we know God's house as the local church. There is also a worldwide church and an eternal church. As His children we belong to a local house in our community. We belong to His church around the world, and we are members of that eternal house that will be finished in the final day. In each of these levels, we find our *special place* that Jesus prepared for us.

No discussion on our heavenly Father would be complete without the understanding of how the church - His house - fits into the divine plan for our lives and how it reveals Him. Concerning our membership in each of these three levels of the Father's house, the local house is of immediate importance to our growth and success. The local house is where our nurturing to maturity takes place. It is in the local house that we begin to see and understand our own special place that Jesus prepared.

What is My Special Place Like?

For we know that if our early house of this tabernacle were dissolved, we have a building of God, an house not made with hands, eternal in the heavens. For in this we groan, earnestly desiring to be clothed upon with our house, which is from heaven:
2 Corinthians 5:1-2 (KJV)

Here is a mystery to our earthly finite minds. Believers who read Jesus' words as recorded in John chapter 14:1, *"I go to prepare a place for you,"* often see His promise as an elaborate mansion with rooms trimmed in gold, filled with fine furnishings and all the comforts offered by an earthly mansion. We see this futuristic place as our retirement home where we will spend the rest of eternity in serene bliss, lounging in the sunlight of the Lord, sipping on the fruit of the vine. This is how I saw my house when I was young in the Lord. This manmade view of our special place in His house and our time in eternity is not only incorrect, but also dangerous to our growth and maturity and our understanding of the Father.

Consider first that our God is a spirit,

God is a Spirit: and they that worship Him must worship Him in spirit and in truth.
John 4:24 (KJV)

His kingdom is a spiritual kingdom not of this world,

"My kingdom is not of this world...
John 18:36a (NIV)

He lives in the realm of the spirit. His house is a spiritual house,

And you are living stones that God is building into his spiritual temple.
1 Peter 2:5a (NLT)

In Hebrews 12:9 Paul called Him, *"the Father of spirits."* And in 1 Corinthians 15:50, Paul writes;

What I am saying, dear brothers and sisters, is that our physical bodies cannot inherit the Kingdom of God. These dying bodies cannot inherit what will last forever. (NLT)

If, therefore, our Father is a spirit, His house is spiritual and only those who are spirit can enter His kingdom, why then do we assume that our special place in His house is anything less than spiritual? And why do we believe that a spiritual mansion is inferior to an earthly mansion?

If God's own house is spiritual, and our special place is in that spiritual house, then our special place must also be spiritual. So then, if our place in His house is spiritual, what is it like? Can we see it? Touch it? Walk in it? The answer is, yes! We see it with spiritual eyes. We touch it with spiritual hands and we walk in it with spiritual feet. There is no other way to experience your mansion in Jesus. This is a tough concept for the natural mind.

> *But people who aren't spiritual can't receive these truths from God's Spirit. It all sounds foolish to them and they can't understand it, for only those who are spiritual can understand what the Spirit means. Those who are spiritual can evaluate all things, but they themselves cannot be evaluated by others.*
> 1 Corinthians 2:14-15 (NLT)

The knowing of our place in His house is a process that begins when we become part of His house here on the earth (the church) If we are faithful to answer the call of His life we will see our place in fullness by the time we depart this world. Jesus already made your place. You must fill it. As Jesus said, *"in my Father's house are many mansions..."* If we are to see our own special place we must begin our search in His house, the church, for that is where our special place is found.

For example, let me tell you about just one of the many special places I have had the honor to experience through the years.

Sam's Place: Sam is a deacon in the church that I pastor. In one word Sam's mansion is, encouragement. This man is living, breathing, encouragement. In the best of times and the most challenging of times, he is ever encouraging. He encourages the poor, the needy, the depressed, the fearful, the desperate, the weary, and the infirmed. When you visit Sam's spiritual house you will go away encouraged. This is what his mansion is made of. The furnishings are words of encouragement that form a place to sit and rest. The walls and ceilings are made of his acts of care and concern that form a covering to those who are exposed to the harsh elements of the world. At his table he serves the wine of the Spirit through his constant prayers for the saints who need refreshing. On Sunday morning when he sings, the contents of his mansion of encouragement spill out all over God's people. This is the mansion that the Lord went to prepare for him. It is a special place where Sam will live throughout his remaining time on this earth and through future eternity. It is unique to him, prepared by Jesus. In fact, it is so unique that if I were to stand in the midst of the congregation and say the word, encouragement, everyone would point to Sam.

Most pastors could go on and on detailing the special places that make up their local churches. In addition to Sam's place, I can note many more such as: *Judy's Place*: the place of motherhood; *Hank's Place*: the place of gentleness; *Jane's Place*: the place of kindness; *Josh's Place*: the place of faithfulness; *Ed's Place*: the place of thoughtfulness; *Eli's Place*: the place of brotherhood. *Anne's Place:* the place of care. And the list goes on. Each of these children of the Father has moved into their mansion and already enjoy the great treasures they have been given. And of course, I only see in part and know in part. The real essence of their place in His house will be seen in fullness at the end of time.

In time, each of us who answer His invitation to enter will be blessed and bless others with the contents of our mansions. Each mansion is a wondrous structure filled with treasures of the kingdom of God that reflect our heavenly Father. Each is built of incorruptible materials that will go with us through eternity. Each is a very special and necessary part of the kingdom of God, and each holds a particular revelation of His nature and character. For this reason, membership in a local church is critical to our development as His children. There is no full revelation of the Father, but by Jesus in His church. Each member carries a part of that revelation. Gathered all together we become the fullness of Jesus, and Jesus is the true revelation of the Father.

And God placed all things under his feet and appointed him to be head over everything for the church, which is the body, the fullness of him who fills everything in every way.
Ephesians 1:21-22 (NIV)

What is your mansion like? What will it be filled with? Well - that is the exciting part of your life in Him - you get to fill it by choosing to love Him today and every day. By becoming all He has destined you to be. In the end it will be filled with the fruit of the love you used here on this earth. If you have loved others - it is already being filled and is showing forth His glory, and at the end of your race it will be even more glorious. Now and through eternity you and your heavenly Father will enjoy your special place together, so much so that He will even call others to see the amazing mansion He built for you.

And God raised us up with Christ and seated us with him in the heavenly realms in Christ Jesus, <u>in order that in the</u>

<u>coming ages he might show the incomparable riches of his grace, expressed in his kindness to us in Christ Jesus.</u>
Ephesians 2:6-7 (NIV)

If you are ready to move in with your Father, then it's time to go to church.

Chapter 15

The Fullness of His House

Six kids! Can you imagine raising six children on one salary? I have no idea how my earthly father and mother did it. There was always food on the table and love for our hearts. When I became the father of four I quickly gained an appreciation for what I once took for granted, simple things like, food, clothes, shelter, and opportunity to learn how to live a good life.

My dad woke early every day at exactly the same time. He went off to work every day, five days a week and almost never missed a day's work in thirty years. He arrived home at exactly 4:30 p.m. every day. He would enter through the side kitchen door and take exactly three steps to the table where he would be seated and begin reading his evening newspaper. When dinner was served he would talk with us about our day. When we all finished eating we were permitted to leave the table. He would rise and walk straight into the living room where he would slide one of his favorite vinyl records into his record player, slip into his favorite chair, and finish reading his paper. All of us kids would be playing around him on the living room floor under his watchful gaze while he listened to Jazz, Gospel, or music from the Big Band era. When he finished his paper he would shower and go directly to bed. By 7:30 p.m. he was fast asleep. And we were all right behind him. On weekends he would take us on picnics or fishing or along with him when he moonlighted as a carpenter. On Sunday we were off to church. I don't believe I ever saw the man do one thing just for himself. He never owned a new car until well after he retired. His joy was being with his babies and he poured everything he had into us.

My dad and mom were our life pillars. The home they provided us, and how they provided it, taught us everything we would ever need to live good lives. But more important, the life they lived in front of us taught us about discipline, character and love. There was a fullness and richness to the home that only can be found at the hands of good parents.

Our heavenly Father also made a good home for us that we can move into today, in this lifetime. He threw open the doors to His earthly home on the Day of Pentecost (that we discussed in chapter 6) when He swept into that upper room to fill His people with His Spirit. This began His church, His house, His temple.

Your local church, God's house, is the Father's provision to us to receive everything we need to grow in the knowledge of Him. In that good home built by His own hands we can grow into the fullness of our relationship to the Father. Under the direction of Jesus, the head of the church, our elder brother, we are nurtured together to the fullness of His stature. We gain opportunity to see all of Him through the revelation that each member of the house brings. As we live and grow together in His house we will eventually become the image of Jesus, and as Jesus himself said, *"if you have seen Me, you have seen the Father."*

In the Father's house we receive provision much the same as an earthly house and family provides for its members. As an earthly father, I willingly provide certain provisions to my family such as the basics of food, clothing, and housing. I also provide the nurturing provisions of instruction, encouragement, fellowship, and safety. In our heavenly Father's house we find the same provisions for life. In the receiving of the provisions

He makes for us we gain great understanding of His heart towards us.

Food to Grow By

With six kids in our house while I was growing up, eating was a competitive sport. And the food was good! When that dinner bell rang it was a stampede to the table and trust me when I say, "*he who was last was never first.*" My dad was a good provider and my mom a great cook. There was always plenty to eat. But the rule was; *if you don't come to the table, you don't eat.*

Every good father provides food for his children. Our spiritual food is served to us at God's banquet table. Those who serve the meals at our Father's table are skilled at preparing the food specifically to meet each of our individual needs. Every feeding is tailored to a believer's age. New believers need milk - the more mature need meat. Those who the Father appoints to feed His children are empowered to prepare and deliver His food accordingly. These servers are called; Apostles, Prophets, Evangelists, Pastors, and Teachers. Their job is to raise-up the children of God.

> *It was he who gave some to be apostles, some to be prophets, some to be evangelists, and some to be pastors and teachers, to prepare God's people for works of service, so that the body of Christ may be built up.*
> Ephesians 4:11-12 (NIV)

Our spiritual meals are served in many ways in His house. They come in the traditional form of preaching and teaching from the pulpit as well as; Sunday school classes, new believer classes, group Bible studies, weekend seminars, retreats, men's and lady's breakfasts, books, audio and video tapes, newsletters, private consultations, the Internet, and the list goes on endlessly. The modern church seems limitless in its creative ways to deliver the milk, bread, and meat of God's word. Suffice it to say that the Lord has made more than ample provision for any child of God who desires to be nourished.

Our part in the feeding process is to get to the dinner table every day, eat, *and* digest what we are served. We get there by faith, believing that the food is important to our growth. We digest by meditating on what is served and by taking the time to study the Word on our own. If we fail to digest we fail to grow. I have witnessed believers suck up sermons week after week without ever digesting what they have eaten at the Lord's table. They fill up every Sunday, but are never nourished. They smile and shake their heads in agreement as the Word is served to them, but never take the time to meditate on it, study it any further or apply it in life. And they never grow in their knowledge of God.

This is a sad testimony especially in light of the elaborate system the Father has provided for our feeding. It is critical we understand that our life with our Father is an endless series of choices. No one in His house can force you to show up at the dinner table. No one can force you to eat. And no one can force you to digest what you decide to eat. These are all your choices. His accountability as a good Father is to make the food available for you. He fulfills this provision through Jesus and His church.

Indeed one can eat up fundamental Christian teachings but never digest, starving for the knowledge of the Father. This stunts growth. The Father has made every provision for our feeding in His house. Jesus Christ has set the banquet table and calls us to eat. So get to a local church, eat and grow. In your growing your life will become rich and full.

New Clothes

I will never forget the day I learned that girl's shirts button up on with the buttons on the left instead of on the right like a boy's shirt. Handing down clothes was a way of life for us growing up. Unfortunately I was the oldest boy, so many of my hand-me-downs came from my two older sisters. No big deal. It was the late sixties. Clothes were cool.

One morning before school I went into my sister's room and borrowed a fine looking brightly striped shirt. It fit me perfectly. I was 13-years-old and my hormones were kicking in big-time. Impressing the girls at school was the order of the day. I slipped on the shirt, pulled on my plaid bell-bottom pants, jumped into my platform shoes and strutted off to school proud as a peacock.

When I dropped down into my homeroom chair the girl seated in front of me immediately took notice, "Cool shirt," she exclaimed, "Did your sister lend it to you?" I was stunned, "Uh..., NO," I retorted in obvious embarrassment. She continued mercilessly, "Why would you buy a girl's shirt?" I had no idea how she knew it was a girl's shirt. "I didn't! It's a boy's shirt," I declared. About this time I started to feel like the Apostle Peter denying Christ three times. "But it buttons on the left," she pointed out. I was trapped, and worse, the girl went right through the school to make sure everyone else knew about my shirt. Ouch. My sister never had to worry about me borrowing her shirts again and I immediately began to petition my mom for a new wardrobe.

When we become God's children we get a complete new wardrobe and, thankfully, don't need to borrow someone's old clothes. These new heavenly garments serve the same purpose in our spiritual lives as natural garments. They offer protection from the elements and demonstrate our new position as His children. But before we can put on this new clothing we must first "put off" the clothing of our old life.

> *put off concerning the former conversation the old man, which is corrupt according to the deceitful lusts; and be renewed in the spirit of your mind; and that ye put on the new man, which after God is created in righteousness and true holiness.*
> Ephesians 4:22-24 (KJV)

The process of putting off the old garments is one that requires personal effort and a lot of help from our brothers and sisters in the Father's house.

When we arrive at the doorstep of our new life we are covered with the filth and death of the earth. Literally we come wrapped in grave clothes. At the point of salvation we are raised from a life of sin and death and given a new garment of righteousness by Jesus. We all go through the process of making this a reality in our lives by willfully putting off the old ways of thinking and living and putting on the new ways of His kingdom. Truly this process can be very intimidating, considering how perfect God is and how imperfect we are.

The important thing to understand is that we are not meant to do it alone. His house on the earth provides older brothers and sisters to help us change our clothes. These are His servants who willingly invest their time and talents into the lives of God's children. From the story of Lazarus being raised from the dead we can see a prophetic glimpse of how these servants assist the Lord in the putting off part of the clothing process;

> *Then Jesus shouted, "Lazarus, come out!" And the dead man came out, his hands and feet bound in graveclothes,*

> his face wrapped in a headcloth. Jesus told <u>them</u>, "Unwrap him and let him go!"
>
> John 11:43-44 (NLT)

The, "THEM," that Jesus called on to unwrap Lazarus were those standing by who answered His request. These are His servants that willfully execute whatever He asks. These brothers and sisters in His house are critical to our changing process.

When we are resurrected into new life through faith in Jesus we are bound up in clothes from the grave of sin. With the burial napkin that covers our face we can barely see the light of His new day. Wrapped in those burial cloths we can barely move. We need help. Those who joyfully give of themselves to help others in God's house assist us in the putting off and putting on processes. Contrary to what many believe this is not accomplished by preaching alone. Preaching and teaching are part of the process, but only small part. Preaching is like opening the door to the closet where the new clothes are hung. Teaching serves to explain the purpose and uses of the new clothes in our daily life. We still need the kind of personal attention that older Christians give to God's newborns and younger children of His house. Through the personal examples and counsel of older Christians, we learn how to put old clothes away (old ways of living) and we learn how to put on the new garments the Lord made available to us (His ways and His thoughts).

My firstborn learned the dressing and undressing process without the benefit of older brothers and sisters. My wife and I invested hours in teaching him how to pull up his pants and put on his shirt by assisting him. He lacked the example of someone his own size and age. To my amazement my second child and third child learned how to dress and undress in half the time. Why? Very simply they saw their older brother do it every day and followed his example. His example did more for his siblings in less time than all our teaching and preaching did for him.

In a local church, brothers and sisters who have gone through the putting off and putting on processes, surround us with their experience and example, and make our clothing process much easier than it would be if we were to try it alone. If you are fortunate to be a member of a church that takes this work seriously, you will find great joy in the changing process.

The clothes themselves are righteousness or, right-ness. This is: thinking right, speaking right and living right. Thinking right is thinking the way our Father thinks. Speaking right is speaking the way He speaks and living right means living the way He created us to live. These are all things that we must learn. These are not things that we are born with or things that magically pop into our lives at the point of our salvation. We learn these things by listening to, observing, and practicing what the Father delivers to us through the fullness deposited in His local church – His house.

The key to how well we learn is in *close living*. When we live together in a house we cannot hide dirty clothes or bad habits. In the confines of that home, we are seen as we really are. When we live this closely, relationships are constantly strained. This straining proves what is in our hearts. The Bible refers to this as, *"iron sharpening iron."* In a good church, brothers and sisters learn how to think, speak, and live together in love. The process of learning through close inescapable relationships with God's children teaches us about righteousness and forces us to put what we learn into action.

Our part in this changing and dressing process is to humbly accept help from those who are sincere and willingly to work with us.

> *In the same way, you younger men must accept the authority of the elders. And all of you, serve each other in humility, for "God opposes the proud but favors the humble."*
> 1 Peter 5:5 (NLT)

Getting spiritually undressed and dressed in the close quarters of a local church is never easy. When a weakness or fault is exposed and confronted, our natural tendency is to react in pride. We either try to cover the fault or run and hide. In a loving gentle house of God this is not necessary. Those who serve in a true representation of God's house will never laugh at, mock, or condemn these revelations, because they themselves have experienced the difficulty of learning in close quarters.

We should never fear exposure. It is only meant for us to see the need for our new clothes. In a good local church *everyone* gets exposed, from the pastor right on down to the newest believer. The process goes on throughout our lives on this earth. No one is exempt, and the new clothing is not optional.

> *when the king came in to see the guests, he noticed a man there who was not wearing wedding clothes. "Friend," he asked, "how did you get in here without wedding clothes?" The man was speechless. The king told the attendants, "Tie him hand and foot, and throw him outside..."*
> Matthew 22:11-13 (NIV)

The worst decision we can make is to run away or hide in fear and pride as mentioned in previous chapters. When we run or hide we miss out on the help that is available to us regarding putting off the old ways and putting on the new. In this cycle of pride we just end up frustrated, always trying to get better on our own. Our heavenly Father never meant for us to undress or dress ourselves as newborns.

Shelter for Our Protection

Every so often in our neighborhood the local bully would seemingly appear out of nowhere, descending on us with his strange desire to pummel us into submission. His arrival always set off a scattering of the neighborhood gang like a flock of geese fleeing a fox that had emerged from the brush. With our feathers flying, our ball-bats abandoned in the street and our bicycle wheels spinning, we were gone in a flash. But that bully never gave up. He would simply zero in on the closest goose and give chase. If he caught you, you were dead-meat. Eventually my dad taught me how to deal with that kid (which we shall not discuss here :) but until then I always knew exactly where to run for safety - home.

In addition to what a house offers inside, a house is also a covering. Its walls and roof protect us from the weather. God's house is a place of refuge from the storms that rage in the world and in our own lives. In the house, while the storms rage outside, we find peace through the comfort of God's Word and in the presence of our family in Christ. We gain encouragement from our brothers and sisters in the house much the same way a child is encouraged and comforted by parents during a thunderstorm (or being chased by a bully). Elder Christians comfort and encourage us through our storms by recounting their own experiences and testimonies. All of this covers our souls and protects us from spiritual weather-damage.

Because thou hast made the LORD, which is my refuge, even the most High, thy habitation; there shall no evil

befall thee, neither shall any plague come nigh thy dwelling. For he shall give his angels charge over thee, to keep thee in all thy ways. They shall bear thee up in their hands, lest thou dash thy foot against a stone.
Psalm 91:9-12 (KJV)

A house is also a place of safety and protection against those in the world who would plot to harm us. Under the watchful eye of caring Christians we are spared the heart-pain and loss of life that befalls those who are led astray by the deceits of darkness. In the house, among our brothers and sisters, we are safe from the tricks of darkness, the lion who lies in wait for God's children in the bushes looking for the young and weak of a flock. Older Christians in the church provide wisdom gained by their own confrontations with this enemy of our souls.

In my lifetime as a child of God I have witnessed literally hundreds of Lone Ranger Christians come in and out of His house and go on to unnecessary destruction as a result of not being a part of a local church. The church is not a man made organization (even if some have made it seem so). The church is a living, God ordained dwelling, bringing us His provision on the earth and revealing our Father's essence. If we fail to come into His refuge place, we are doomed by our own stubborn pride and we never come to the better life He offers.

Teachers to Build Us Up

My mom and dad were great teachers. I learned something new from them every day. My mom taught me how to care for my brothers and sisters and how to see life as an opportunity to do great things. My dad taught me how to invest my life into the only things that last forever – other people and God.

The church is a place where the Father takes opportunity to make investment of Himself into us. He does this by providing men and women who are willing to lay down their own lives in service to His church. This divine provision comes to us through what is often referred to as the, Five-Fold Ministries.

True five-fold ministry people are dedicated and appointed (chosen) by God. They are titled: Apostles, Prophets, Evangelists, Pastors, and Teachers. These are living gifts from God to His people. Their purpose, as noted in Paul's letter to the Ephesians, chapter 4, is, "*to build up the church.*"

These are people who the Father calls, trains, and sets apart for the express purpose of doing His nurturing work amongst us. Through great sacrifice, tribulation, sufferings, and faith they have come to see and understand the heart of the Father toward His children. Each of the five ministries express His divine direction and purpose in very specific ways so that each of us can come to the full understanding of who He is and what He desires.

These gifts take us from birth, through infancy, childhood, puberty, and on to adulthood in our spiritual lives. Simply put they execute the nurturing of God's children. Through these brothers and sisters, by Jesus, and the Holy Spirit, the Father teaches us and preserves us until the time that we can each stand on our own in full maturity. These gifts are divine provision for our growth in our knowledge of Him.

This ordained church leadership is not optional to us. If we fail to recognize these gifts, and draw back from them in fear of being hurt by humans, or simply rebel against the idea of being humbled in front of others, we become doomed to living our life small. Many gifted people come into Jesus' new life with a great zeal to serve God, but refuse to submit to the order that He set into His own house. By trying to do it outside of the

Father's order they fall prey to the wiles of the enemy. They suffer lost opportunity, the church suffers the loss of their presence, and those outside God's house lose the light that their life testimony and gifts could have supplied.

The five ministries listed in Ephesians chapter 4 are gifts from God. To benefit from them we must receive them in faith and open the gifts by opening our hearts in faith to them. The great danger in this, of course, revolves around the fact that these gifts are contained inside imperfect human packages. I believe, however, that if a believer sincerely puts his or her trust in the gift rather than in the man or woman carrying the gift, the Lord will never fail to deliver.

Gifts & Ministries to Help Us

If you can picture the Five-Fold Ministries as executing the role of nurturing in His church, then the *Gifts and Ministries* can be seen as the workers that make a house function in fullness.

As a parent my overall duty is to see that my children are raised up to maturity. In the working of that role, I appoint each member of our house certain duties and roles that help express my desires and execute the building up of the house. My eldest son was accountable to protect and oversee his younger brother and sisters when I was not there. My middle son was given opportunity to teach and encourage his younger sisters. My eldest daughter was assigned to receiving guests. My youngest child had authority to answer the phone. Each child has a part to play in ministering to the family and home. Each part is important. Each works to strengthen the whole. Each has responsibility delegated down from me in whatever way I see fit as the head of the house.

Similarly the Gifts and Ministries that are part of God's house are given according to God's own choices. Each member of His house is given a gift and or ministry intended for everyone's profit.

> *the manifestation of the Spirit is given to every man to profit withal ...all these worketh that one and the selfsame Spirit, dividing to every man severally as he will... but now hath God set the members every one of them in the body, as it hath pleased Him.*
> 1 Corinthians 12:7,11,18 (KJV)

As is stated these gifts (though different) all work towards the fullness of the working of His Spirit. Each gift and ministry adds divine provision needed to build up and mature the church into the fullness of the knowledge of God.

Space does not permit to review of all the gifts and ministries mentioned in the scriptures. There are many fine books written on this subject for anyone interested in searching them out. The important issues are that they are given for our profit, each of us has a gift, and they all work to reveal His love to us. These gifts and ministries are to be used under the authority of the local church for the sake of order, and they are to be used only as tools that help us grow in the knowledge of Him.

The church is the place that the Lord finds expression of these gifts and ministries. They become an expression of His love working in our midst and in that a revelation of our Father on this earth. You have something special for the local church you attend. Something that can help to build up your church family while they are here on the earth. And each person's gift brings a revelation, in part, of our Father. Being part of a good gift-filled church is a great benefit in our journey to know Him.

***

A local house of God is His mercy and grace to our lives. The Father loves his children and desires that not even one be lost. In the church we are safe. In the church we learn our Father's heart. Once again, our part revolves around choices. The cover, safety and food are there. To take advantage of this provision, we must remain inside the church, responding and taking part in healthy relationships. We cannot expect to be safe if we are constantly running in and out of fellowship with the church. By fellowship I mean more than simply attending church each Sunday. I am referring to an intimate intermingling of your life with the life of the local body of Christ. Those who refuse to become sincerely involved in the lives of His family are doomed to remain on the fringe of the flock. The sheep on the outer fringe are the first to be eaten by predators, but those in the family of God, who sincerely love one another, gain the knowledge of their good Father and the better life of knowing Him.

Chapter 16

In His Fellowship

I was tired, irritable and just had no desire to get out of bed. I desperately needed to be encouraged but I had absolutely no desire to talk with anyone about anything. I was pouting – feeling sorry for myself. Things had just not gone the way I wanted the day before. I yanked the blankets up over my head in defiance. Just about then that still-small-voice of the Holy Spirit whispered, "Get up." (It's amazing how loud that still-small-voice can be at times.) Grudgingly I tossed the covers aside and dragged myself to life. It's really hard to skip church when you're the pastor.

Living close to the front-line of life's battlefields can become a burden to the soul when we don't release everything to God's care each day. On that morning I was just that person, worrying and fretting through the week until I was just tapped out by Sunday morning.

I didn't get much further than the front foyer of the church meeting hall before my friends saw right into my soul. They smiled, slapped me on the back, quoted scriptures to me, hung up my coat and they dug relentlessly into my heart until they knew exactly what the problem was and fixed it. Before I began to preach that day, I had been lifted up from my pit by the fellowship of those saints. I preached one of the greatest sermons of my life and went home happy. They worked the sincere fellowship of God's house into me.

We've already mentioned that the body of Christ, the church, contains *all the fullness of Him.* (Ephesians 1:23) The real treasure of that fullness lies in the fellowship of those who *are* the house – His people.

When we think of Christian fellowship we imagine a group of people standing around in the church hall after a Sunday service sipping coffee, laughing, and enjoying each other's company. But the enjoyment of each other's company is only the result, or by-product, of fellowship. In other words, this is a benefit of fellowship. This is not the powerful fellowship described in the scriptures. Consider what the scriptures teach us about true fellowship.

Our fellowship is in Jesus;

God is faithful, by whom ye were called unto the fellowship of His Son Jesus Christ our Lord.
1 Corinthians 1:9 (KJV)

The word, *fellowship*, here is from the Greek word, koinonia, which is defined as; communion, a sharing in common, a share in, an association or partnership. True fellowship is based on something that two people have in common. True fellowship, which His church offers us, must revolve around each of our relationships through Christ with the Father. True fellowship, as described in the scriptures, is based on the fact that we (His children) have one thing in common: Jesus Christ and our Father. Around this point we fellowship.

That which was from the beginning, which we have heard, which we have seen with our eyes, which we have looked upon, and our hands have handled, of the Word of life; ... That which we have seen and heard declare we unto you, that ye also may have fellowship with us: and truly our

> *fellowship is with the Father, and with His Son Jesus Christ.*
> 1 John 1:1,3 (KJV)

The key to benefiting from the true fellowship found in the church is to realize that we are each a shareholder in the Lord. We each have part of Him. When we gather together as His church, all the parts combine to become *all the fullness of Him*, as mentioned in Ephesians 1:23. Each believer carries a special inherited part that we received by the death and resurrection of Jesus. Each of us was given a down payment, a foretaste, of our complete inheritance when the Spirit entered us at salvation.

> *This signet from God is the first installment on what's coming, a reminder that we'll get everything God has planned for us, a praising and glorious life.*
> Ephesians 1:14 (The Message)

The Apostle Paul, who was writing there in Ephesians, went on to tell the readers that it was his greatest desire and prayer that they come to the full revelation of what they were called to *AND* the riches available to us in the saints:

> *I pray that the eyes of your heart may be enlightened, so that you may know what is the hope of His calling, what are the riches of the glory of His inheritance in the saints.*
> Ephesians 1:18 (NAS)

Paul's prayer for them was that they would come to see and understand what was available to them, "in the saints." It was later in that chapter that he declared the church to be the fullness of Christ.

Fellowship means so much more than giggles of gladness between two believers. Fellowship is not something we do but rather something we have. When we are born into His kingdom we are born into fellowship. In that position of holding a part of the whole we become a critical part of the fullness intended for the church.

Therefore, fellowship, in its true sense, means to be a partaker, a sharer, in who and what He is. If we are not sharing the part we have we are *not* fellowshipping! To be part of the fellowship of the saints we must share with the entire church! If you are not sharing your part, you are not a partaker; you are only a taker. If you are attending a local church only to take whatever you can get for your own betterment you are not in fellowship. If you come in and go out every week without investing that special part of your Father's character that is special in you - then you are little more than a visitor. Selfish fellowship is not fellowship at all. To really be in fellowship and gain the benefits of it we must love our brothers and sisters by sharing our own special place (mansion) We cannot know God or fellowship with Him if we do not lay down our own lives for our brothers and sisters in His house.

No one has ever seen God. But if we love each other, God lives in us, and his love is brought to full expression in us.
1 John 4:12 (NLT)

When everyone is sharing, the church grows to maturity and prospers. When we are part of that process we mature and prosper ourselves.

but speaking the truth in love, we are to grow up in all aspects into Him, who is the head, even Christ, from whom the whole body, being fitted and held together by that

which every joint supplies, according to the proper working of each individual part, causes the growth of the body for the building up of itself in love.
Ephesians 4:15-16 (NAS)

When we hold back our part we all suffer;

If one part suffers, all the parts suffer with it, and if one part is honored, all the parts are glad. All of you together are Christ's body, and each of you is a part of it.
1 Corinthians 12:26-27 (NLT)

For this reason, selfish fellowship is either very immature, or in the case of older saints who should know better, shallow. You are a critical part of the Father's provision for His children. If you do not share what He has given to you, you rob your brothers and sisters, and Him, of that special part, and, you rob yourself of getting to know Him.

To receive the benefits of fellowship in His house, begin sharing what you have. Before you can fully receive fellowship (the inheritance) that is found in others, you must give. And according to the measure you give of yourself to others it will be measured back to you.

"Give, and you will receive. Your gift will return to you in full—pressed down, shaken together to make room for more, running over, and poured into your lap. The amount you give will determine the amount you get back."
Luke 6:38 (NLT)

Considering then that true fellowship refers to sharing our part and receiving parts that others hold, we now come to the true value of fellowship and its purpose in our life with our Father.

Fellowship with the people of His church is the vehicle that brings us to gain the fullness of our Father's kingdom. We give a part – we receive a part. The more we give of the inheritance He gave us, the more we receive of that inheritance from other depositories in His treasure house; the body of Christ, the church.

From one part we receive the wisdom of the Father, from another the gentleness of the Father, from another the compassion of the Father, from another the kindness of the Father, from another the long-suffering, from another patience, from another humility, from another selflessness, from another perseverance, and the list goes on infinitely. By living in the position of true fellowship (which Jesus purchased for us with His blood) we get to see, hear, touch, smell and taste the fullness of our heavenly Father. As we live together in that fellowship, sharing our portion one with the other, we gain the power of those divine qualities in our own life.

A good example of this can be seen in the lives of a husband and wife. When a man and woman marry they come together with two different personalities. But as time passes their personalities begin to mingle. Each takes on certain character traits of the other as a result of living (fellowshipping) together closely. The more they spend time together in this union the more they become alike. This process is irresistible. It happens naturally as a result of living together.

This is how godly fellowship works in those who become part of the lives of others in the Father's house. When I say, become a part of their lives, I don't mean having tea and cookies together once a week or going to a ballgame together or sitting about gossiping about the faults of others. I am referring to a commitment of love that is worked out through genuine concern over, and investment in, the lives of others in His church according to His pattern. Shedding blood, sweat and tears for others.

True fellowship is a choice of sacrificial love. To fellowship in the church requires the same level of commitment common to a marriage. It means being a part of, a partner, a sharer, of everything. You must commit your part totally, through good times and bad, for richer or poorer, in sickness and in health. In fact the very pinnacle of fellowship is found only when we love others enough to fellowship in their sufferings, tribulations and yes - even their weaknesses.

And, it is not only the giving of yourself but also the receiving from others that is critical to fellowship. If you are too proud to receive from others you will never experience sincere fellowship. Everyone in your local church has something to give you that you need! Even the smallest child has at least a gentle smile to share with you.

The Best Fellowship

Now you can see the mistake of limiting your understanding of fellowship to chatting after a church meeting or watching a football game together on a Sunday afternoon. The best fellowship takes place when the church, or a single member, is under heavy attack. When everyone is being pressed closely together. When iron is clashing against iron. In those seasons we are forced to give out of our own part beyond measure and very often must humbly rely on the parts offered by others. This is true love and true fellowship. It is the place where true saints are seen and imposters are exposed. It is in this pressure cooker of fellowship that we find the greatest of our Father's fellowship. It is here that we truly find the revelation of His heart of hearts is revealed to us all.

Greater love hath no man than this, that a man lay down his life for his friends.
John 15:13 (KJV)

But rejoice, inasmuch as ye are partakers of Christ's sufferings; that, when his glory shall be revealed, ye may be glad also with exceeding joy.
1 Pet 4:13 (KJV)

If you are not part of a good local church, consider finding one. And when I say, local church, I mean a church based in your area, your hometown where you live, where everyone knows everyone else. This is where great intimacy breeds life best and where the greatest revelation of our Father can be found.

Chapter 17

In His Light

Have you ever noticed how quickly a fire draws a crowd? When I was very young our local community collected spent Christmas trees from each home after the holidays and, after stacking them in a huge pile near the town park, they would dispose of them by burning them in a giant bonfire. In a community of three thousand homes you can imagine the bonfire this created. Shortly after the fire was lit the people of the town would begin showing up by the hundreds to just stand and watch.

At some point in time this tradition ended, but I vividly remember how this annual fire would draw everyone to the park. Looking back today it seems a bit silly to think that we were all drawn to what was essentially a giant garbage fire. But this is a good example of how fire can draw people.

Consider the crowd that would be drawn to a bonfire that never goes out, a fire that burns continually, shedding warmth and light but never consuming the fuel supply. This would truly be an amazing sight.

This is the call of the house of God. This fire was started with the death and resurrection of Jesus, and it is growing every day. One day soon this house fire will draw millions across the earth to its light.

Consider Jesus' words concerning His mission on the earth as He prepared to go to the Cross:

"I have come to bring fire on the earth, and how I wish it were already kindled!"
Luke 12:49 (NIV)

There was a passion to this statement. Jesus (and the Father) could not wait for the fire to begin. They were excited at what the fire would do. Here is that fire:

> *Ye are the light of the world. A city that is set on a hill cannot be hid. Neither do men light a candle, and put it under a bushel, but on a candlestick; and it giveth light unto all that are in the house. Let your light so shine before men, that they may see your good works, and glorify your Father which is in heaven.*
> Matthew 5:14-16 (KJV)

Every saint is part of the fire. One flame among many flames. The fire began at Pentecost landing upon the heads of the new church after Jesus' resurrection.

> *And when the day of Pentecost was fully come, they were all with one accord in one place. And suddenly there came a sound from heaven as of a rushing mighty wind, and it filled all the house where they were sitting. And there appeared unto them cloven tongues like as of fire, and it sat upon each of them.*
> Acts 2:1-3 (KJV)

Glory! The fire that the Father had prepared for us through thousands of years was kindled! This was a house fire like none before and none after! Through the disciples, the Lord set up His house. At Pentecost, He put a torch to it! And the fire immediately drew the people.

> *At that time there were devout Jews from every nation living in Jerusalem. When they heard the loud noise,*

everyone came running, and they were bewildered to hear their own languages being spoken by the believers
Acts 2:5-6 (NLT)

Right off the bat God's fire drew a crowd! This is what the church, His house, means to those who are on the outside. It is a beacon, an amazing light that burns for all to see and be drawn to.

Consider that you are one flame, a candle. What happens when a hundred, two hundred, or a thousand candles are pressed together in one place? A fire! A big fire! A bright light!

A single candle alone is good for giving light to one or two people at a time. This is our call as individual believers. We shine our light to each person we meet. But together, with our brothers and sisters, our candles combine to shine a wide beacon to many. This is the outward working of the church. The heavenly Father has set up a bright light, a beacon for all to see so that they might turn their lives away from darkness to His marvelous light and that He can have them with Him in safety. What a great revelation of His master plan of love for us.

Our lives are fused in fellowship with the lives of the people of our local church and then from there fused to the entire worldwide church. In this, our talents and treasures become intertwined into a powerful light that grows brighter each day. The more each candle offers, the brighter the light becomes. The brighter the light becomes the more it can be seen by those in darkness. When an entire local church is fused in the unity of true fellowship, the fire becomes irresistibly powerful. When this happens entire communities are consumed by the brightness of the fire. The Prophet Isaiah foretold the power of this holy fire in the church:

"ARISE, SHINE; for your light has come, And the glory of the Lord has risen upon you. "For behold, darkness will cover the earth, And deep darkness the peoples; But the Lord will rise upon you, And His glory will appear upon you. "And nations will come to your light, And kings to the brightness of your rising. "Lift up your eyes round about, and see; they all gather together, they come to you.
Isaiah 60:1-4 (NAS)

The church is destined for this glory! This is what you and your local church can be part of! It is happening now! It WILL come to its fullness. It spreads like wild fire. In local churches that have answered the call to nurture and mature its members, this is already a reality. In the years to come more of these local *houses on fire* will spring up around the country and around the world.

This is why Jesus excitedly wished that the fire were already kindled. Jesus was looking beyond the Cross - through the day of Pentecost - to our day when the flames would become a raging, all consuming, bonfire casting light to all men. Why were He and the Father so excited? Simple. They knew the light of the fire would bring many more children to the house of the Father and bring the completion of His new dwelling place! Everything goes back to that one divine passion; He wants to be with us all!

This holy fire, which shines from the church, means everything to those who do not yet know the salvation of Jesus. They are in a dark cold place. We are the light that comes out of heaven. Together in His church we combine to become the fullness of that light, a vision of our God. When the fullness of the light shines it will shine into *ALL* the darkness that is on the earth, into every soul in every man and woman. The beacon from this light will draw them to the door of eternal life. It is their chance at finding the Father. Let us not forsake nor be slack concerning our accountability in this labor.

As noted in Paul's letter to the Ephesians, the church, when it is grown, becomes the image of Jesus on the earth:

> *It was he who gave some to be apostles, some to be prophets, some to be evangelists, and some to be pastors and teachers, to prepare God's people for works of service, so that the body of Christ may be built up until we all reach unity in the faith and in the knowledge of the Son of God and become mature, attaining to the whole measure of the fullness of Christ.*
> Ephesians 4:11-13 (NIV)

What is your part? *STEP INTO THE FIRE!* Rise up today. Every local church can have the vision of God's purposes in this hour. Invest your flame into the flame of others with like minds in the place that your heavenly Father planted you. Once you step into the fellowship of the light you will never be the same, and your investment will change the lives of others forever.

What do we gain? That fire, made of everyone's candle throughout time, is the perfect revelation of the Father. In that fire, as part of it, we see Him from the inside. From that fresh vantage point our perspective of life changes, enabling us to grow in the knowledge of Him and resulting in a greater portion of His fellowship. Glory!

Chapter 18

Eternal Opportunities

In my lifetime I have known a lot of people who did, *good things*, but never loved God's people. They did works for His kingdom but neglected true fellowship with His people. I once knew of a man who did mighty healings and supernatural wonders but immediately following the service would offend and ignore church members who cried out for personal attention. This should not be so. Anyone can work miracles in the name and power of the Lord! But those who truly know Him can work the miracle of true love. Everything else is only a dim reflection of Him.

Salvation through Jesus truly brings us many good things from our Father. Along with these great gifts comes ever-increasing opportunity. Before we finish this section on life in His house it would be a good time to discuss the opportunity we have to move the eternal heart of our Father. Our actions in His house will be paramount to us on the final judgment day and critical to our growth today in our understanding of our Father.

We know that through Christ Jesus our sins have been forgiven,

> *Giving thanks unto the Father, which hath made us meet to be partakers of the inheritance of the saints in the light: Who hath delivered us from the power of darkness, and hath translated us into the kingdom of His dear Son: In whom we have redemption through His blood even the forgiveness of sins.*

Colossians 1:12-14 (KJV)

We also know that because of Jesus our sins are removed from us as far as the east is from the west,

> *As far as the east is from the west, so far hath He removed our transgressions from us.*
> Psalms 103:12 (KJV)

If this is so, what will we be judged on in the end and what will our reward be based upon?

Those who never accept the sacrifice of Jesus' blood will of course be judged according to their sins. When they arrive at the final judgment, they will be covered in sin. Because they refused the initial gift of salvation they will be sent away forever into eternal death. But those who arrive washed by the blood of Jesus will also be judged.

Many people are under the delusion that their good works will be the key to their judgment. But this is clearly not the case as noted in Matthew 7:21-23,

> *Not everyone that saith unto me, Lord, Lord, shall enter into the kingdom of heaven; but he that doeth the will of my Father which is in heaven. Many will say to me in that day, Lord, Lord, have we not prophesied in thy name? and in thy name have cast out devils? and in thy name done many wonderful works? And then I will profess unto them, I never knew you: depart from me, ye that work iniquity.*
> (KJV)

Consider carefully Jesus' response to their cries. He told them to get away because, *"He never knew them."* But they had prophesied for Him and cast out demons for Him, healed the sick, did miracles and raised up other wonderful works for Him! BUT THEY MISSED IT ALL! This is not what our lives in Christ are about! This is not what it means to be a child of the Father. These are only things we do while we are on the earth. In and of themselves, they mean very little! In and of themselves they are worth little! You can stack up all the good works in the world and they are still meaningless if we have not done them in the will of our Father.

If these good works are not His complete will, then what is His will? What is it that proves our place in His kingdom? How do we come to know that He knows us? I for one do not want to wait until that judgment day to find out! Thank God we don't need to wait. We can know now.

Think on this – if His entire plan through history is based on His love for us and His desire for our fellowship, then should it not be reasonable for His final judgment of the saints to be based on the same principles of love and fellowship?

Look at the commands of Jesus,

A new commandment I give unto you, That ye should love one another; as I have loved you, that ye also love one another. By this shall all men know that ye are my disciples, if ye have love one to another.
John 13:34-35 (KJV)

If ye keep my commandments ye shall abide in my love . . . This is my commandment, That ye love one another, as I have loved you.
John 15:10, 12 (KJV)

This is how we are judged: by how we have loved Him! Love is what it is all about! Not good works or much knowledge! These things are only the tools we use to love. The real issue is how much, if at all, we loved Him! How do we love Him? By loving His children, our brothers and sisters in His house! Consider this second declaration of how that Day of Judgment will unfold,

> *"But when the Son of Man comes in his glory, and all the angels with him, then he will sit upon his glorious throne. All the nations will be gathered in his presence, and he will separate the people as a shepherd separates the sheep from the goats. He will place the sheep at his right hand and the goats at his left. "Then the King will say to those on his right, 'Come, you who are blessed by my Father, inherit the Kingdom prepared for you from the creation of the world. For I was hungry, and you fed me. I was thirsty, and you gave me a drink. I was a stranger, and you invited me into your home. I was naked, and you gave me clothing. I was sick, and you cared for me. I was in prison, and you visited me.' "Then these righteous ones will reply, 'Lord, when did we ever see you hungry and feed you? Or thirsty and give you something to drink? Or a stranger and show you hospitality? Or naked and give you clothing? When did we ever see you sick or in prison and visit you?' "And the King will say, 'I tell you the truth, when you did it to one of the least of these my brothers and sisters, you were doing it to me!'*
> Matthew 25:31-45 (NLT)

This makes our judgment clear. We are not judged by the works themselves, but by how the deeds served and built up our Christian brothers and sisters in this life. This is understandable in light of the fact that everything the Father does is for His children. If we really love Him then we will love what He loves! He loves people. He loves His children.

Our love of Him is proven out in this life by how much we have responded to the needs of our brothers and sisters in Christ. If we do not sincerely love His children, all of our other actions mean very little.

> *If I speak with the tongues of men and of angels, but do not have love, I have become a noisy gong or a clanging cymbal. And if I have the gift of prophecy, and know all mysteries and all knowledge, and if I have all faith, so as to remove mountains, but do not have love, I am nothing. And if I give all my possessions to feed the poor, and if I deliver my body to be burned, but do not have love, it profits me nothing.*
> I Corinthians 13:1-3 (NAS)

In the end we will be judged by how much we have loved Him by loving His people. (those who are saved by Christ and are living His life) Do not miss this point! Good works to mankind in general do not qualify! These acts are expected of us (and we should all love our neighbors as we love ourselves) but they are not the core issue. The scriptures clearly state that it is the love of His brothers and sisters that proves our love for Him and proves our faith in Him. This proof, alone, is the beginning of our judgment. Not ministries, or knowledge, or works of faith, or church attendance, or giving and tithing.

The Bible tells us exactly how we can be sure of our salvation. There is a real, visible measuring rod of our salvation and maturity noted in the word of God,

If we love our Christian brothers and sisters, it proves that we have passed from death to life. But a person who has no love is still dead.
1 John 3:14 (NLT)

This is the proof that assures us today and is our evidence at the Day of Judgment.

Understand this principle of loving the children of God. The degree of quality by which we follow His love today will determine our reward tomorrow. All of our works will be judged for that quality,

Each man's work will become evident; for the day will show it, because it is to be revealed with fire; and the fire itself will test the quality of each man's work.
1 Corinthians 3:13 (NAS)

So consider this - you can tithe ten percent of your next paycheck to the work of the Lord, but if you know that someone in the church needs to borrow ten dollars from you that week and you refuse, you have done nothing. You can get up tomorrow morning, sell all your possessions and give the money to the local food bank, but if you refused to encourage a downhearted sister in Christ the day before, your generosity means little. You can be the greatest worker at your church this week, but if you are too proud or too busy to stop and talk to a younger Christian church member, you missed the treasure of the eternal opportunity to know God and have Him know you.

If God only wanted servants He could have made them from the rocks of the earth. He did not create you to be just a servant. Service to God is a free will choice. It is expected from sons and daughters living in a house. Your higher call as His child is to love Him. To love Him is to love His people. Not some of His people or the ones who you THINK are His people or the ones who are easy to love, or the ones who agree with your doctrines, but ALL of His people! Good, bad or ugly; no matter, they are in Him by the blood sacrifice of Jesus. In the end those who are and are not will be plainly seen. Until then we are to judge nothing.

> *Therefore judge nothing before the appointed time; wait till the Lord comes. He will bring to light what is hidden in darkness and will expose the motives of men's hearts.*
> 1 Corinthians 4:5 (NIV)

I have listened to many believers attempt to justify their separation from fellowship with God's people. The most common excuses are; "Those people are not very fun," "They are not mature enough for me," "They are too harsh," "Someone offended me," "They want too much from me," "They are too spiritual for me," "They do not offer me and my family enough activities," "I'm not getting fed like I would like." But there is no acceptable reason for separating our hearts from His people. How can we claim to love anyone if we are so easily moved to abandon the children of God? On this love we will be judged. In this love we find amazing opportunity to please our Father.

If the King's greatest passion is His love for His people, it can be expected that He will judge all things in the light of that love. Those who love His children are judged well. Those who despise them, hate or care not for them are judged to death.

The only things that will pass into eternity with us are those things that are eternal. Do not fall for the deception that a big picture screen is going to roll down at the judgment and our great works will be replayed in stereo. What will be the evidence presented on that day? Eternal things! What are the eternal things? YOU ARE ETERNAL – HIS CHILDREN ARE ETERNAL – HIS LOVE IS ETERNAL – HE IS ETERNAL. And that is it! The earth and everything on it is temporal. Ministries, gifts and knowledge are temporary. These will all pass but love will remain and pass into eternity with us and only our acts of love will be there as seen in those who stand there with us who we have loved. There will only be a record of who you have loved in His house, how you loved them and what that love accomplished. Those standing there, His children whom you have loved, will be the *eternal evidence* of your love. Think on that. If you have not personally loved any of His children in this life there will be nothing there to prove you are one of His. And if there is no eternal evidence of your love, He may declare that He does not know you. If there are many people there on that day to testify of your love, you will be rewarded accordingly. It is that simple. You can't drag out your wonderful works and miracles on that day! The only thing you can show will be the evidence of your love that is found in the eternal souls of His people. Even if it's just kindness to the last child of God you see standing at your deathbed begging you for forgiveness. At least you loved one. Who knows? He is a very merciful God.

    I once listened as a zealous young man visiting our church described his plans to fulfill his life's dream of being a missionary. He told me all about the nation he was going to and the wonderful works that he planned to be part of but never once mentioned his love of the people in that land. Bless his soul. I prayed the Lord would use him and eventually He did after a few adjustments to his heart. As he spoke I couldn't help but to feel the groaning of the heart of his Father. The dream is good, but the motive is wrong. We should never minister because it is our dream, but because we are driven by our love for Him and His people. This is the kind of work that issues out of the heart of our Father. This work bears eternal fruit.

There is a judgment coming that will be both terrible and glorious. Each of us who call ourselves Christians will be there. Some will pass into glory on that day with the ones we have loved. Others will be turned out to eternal loneliness, as they have lived their lives.

Those who love Him now, in this life, by loving His people are already fulfilling His eternal desire, gaining opportunity to know Him better and ensuring eternal reward. Those who refuse to be part of His people's lives are already judged and living in darkness, in spite of what they say with their mouths concerning faith. The Father does not desire that any be lost but He will be forced to condemn many in the end because they refuse to love Him today by investing in and caring for the lives of His children.

The practical out-working of loving Him by loving His people, once again goes back to fellowship. His people are His church. In His house we live with them, serve them, suffer with them and rejoice with them. This is how we love His people and this is how we love Him. When we love the people of His house and labor with them in His fields, we in turn love Him. In the end we will be rewarded according to how much fruit we produced in the lives of those we led into His kingdom and those we loved in His house. In that process we come to a better life now by loving what He loves.

To have full fellowship with Him we must think in, and live in, this truth because this is what He is always thinking and talking about; His children. If we fail to pursue this common ground we can never fellowship with Him, we will never truly come to know Him, and His light is not in us.

If anyone claims, "I am living in the light," but hates a Christian brother or sister, that person is still living in darkness.
1 John 2:9 (NLT)

If no light is found in us at the end of our life, we will go to everlasting darkness. But if there is proof of light on that day, you will be welcomed into the kingdom that was prepared for us since before the foundation of the world. And the Lord will say, "Well Done!"

As you can see, our life in His house is full of good things and great opportunities. It is also the place where we have opportunity to express our love to Jesus and our Father. With the treasure comes accountability. Let us never fail to understand the value that our God puts upon His children. To love the children of His house is to love Him. And in loving His children we walk side-by-side with Him, learning and growing in His knowledge.

PART FIVE

WITH HIM IN HIS FIELDS

Do you want to learn to serve your heavenly Father and really get to know Him? Find the lowest, dirtiest and most unrewarding job you can spot in your church and volunteer to oversee it.

Chapter 19

The Farmer's Children

My wife is descended from a long line of hard-working farmers. Her grandparents and great-grandparents farmed the fertile hills and valleys of Pennsylvania. In her mother's family there were twelve children. For a farmer this was a typical family.

Farming is tough work. Farmers rely on their children for labor. Farm children are trained to work in their father's trade from a very early age. They do the will of their father in service to his farm. The reward for a child's faithful service to adulthood was a portion of the land and stock for their own use. The father's land and wealth became the land and wealth of the children who obediently served and did his will. Upon coming to this inheritance the farmer's children were given a special parcel where they could have their own home constructed. They were still with the father, but also had their own special place.

When we come to our new life in our heavenly Father's kingdom, we are born into all the wealth of His land. From a very early age we are expected to grow and learn of His ways and follow in His footsteps. We are called upon to do His work in His fields. As we grow to maturity in doing His will, we come to see and understand our inheritance and gain the fullness of our own special place in His kingdom. This investment into His farm is expected of us the same as an earthly farmer expects his natural children to serve in the work of his farm.

Child Servants – Heirs and Sons

One of the richest men to live in America made a practice of putting his children out onto the assembly lines of his factories to work alongside his employees without special privileges. The result was that all of his children went on to be successful on their own. His children were his heirs. He could have easily pampered them and treated them to the fullness of their inheritance at any time. But in wisdom he gave them the greater gift of experience. As a result they learned their father's business from the ground up and learned the principles of *his* success for themselves. In the end they possessed not only their father's physical wealth, but also the wealth of his nature and character, and in that they lived better lives. They were made full.

This is the course that our heavenly Father presses us into following a short period of babying after our new birth into His house. The intent of this training by experience is to give us opportunity to gain not only the wealth of His house, but also the full knowledge of His ways and His nature as they are revealed in His works. When we come to know His ways our lives improve dramatically.

When we enter God's house through salvation we become legal heirs of our heavenly Father. This is our birthright. By the blood sacrifice of Jesus Christ we are born into this position.

Salvation is, however, progressive. We go through that *putting off* of the old man and a *putting on* of the new man. In spite of the fact that legally, before the heavens, we are heirs, we have yet to secure the full experience of that reality while we are still growing in His ways. The training and teaching processes that we discussed in earlier chapters are the vehicles that bring us to what we have legally gained through Jesus.

In the beginning of our understanding we are sons and daughters by birth. But in the workings of His farm we are trained much like a servant hired to work the fields.

Now I say, That the heir, <u>as long as he is a child,</u> differeth nothing from a servant, though he be lord of all;
Galatians 4:1 (KJV)

Many new believers come to the Father's house with great expectations of supernatural pampering and golden goblets filled with treasure. It is not long, however, until they find themselves knee deep in sheep dip being handed a supernatural shovel. This is the true heritage of a farmer's children. This is our heritage as children of the heavenly Father.

Our Lord is a shepherd. He has sheep. Sheep are not neat, clean or nestled in the arms of the gentle shepherd like those depicted in religious paintings. Sheep get filthy if left to themselves. They stray easily. They are often stubborn and can be dangerous. They are tough to raise and tough to lead.

Our Lord is a farmer of the land. Our service to the master gardener is often dirty and hard but the result is wisdom and knowledge in the ways of His life. Farming the land is one of the most demanding of jobs. From morning to night a farmer wrestles with tilling, fertilizing, weeding, planting, watering and harvesting. Three hundred sixty five days a year covered with dust, dirt, mud and sweat.

God is also a builder. He builds each of us up individually and together into a temple. Building is hard labor. A builder must haul, cut, shape, hammer and mold raw materials into a usable structure. Through rain, snow, searing heat and frigid cold, a builder invests tirelessly into the progress of his building.

This is the character of our Father and Lord. This is the work that He has called each of His children to do on His behalf. As His children, this is our heritage. We are born into these trades. Living in His house we are expected to invest in His work. Service to Him not only brings Him glory, but also brings us to maturity and a full knowledge of the heart of our Father. I learned more about my earthly father working alongside him than in all my other activities with Him. This is our birthright in our heavenly Father's house and is the fastest way to get to know Him intimately.

Chapter 20

Advancement by Faithfulness

My life as a pastor began in the toilets. Literally.

I was born into my heavenly Father's kingdom at the age of eighteen. After a few years of running the fringes of His church, I settled into a local ministry that was using an old theater house as a meeting hall. We gathered there every Sunday. On Fridays and Saturdays a local theatrical group, which used the theater before our Sunday morning service, always left the premises in a state of disaster. Half empty beer cans littered the floors. Cigarette butts were strewn about. Waste paper covered the restroom floors and the toilets were always overflowing and usually covered with the fruits of alcoholic overindulgence. Forgive the graphic description, but this is a clear depiction of where I began.

For a period of two years I swept those floors, bagged those beer cans and mopped up indescribable filth in service to the Lord's work in that place. I usually did it alone or with the help of one other person, and seldom received recognition for it. I did, however, receive recognition from my Father in Heaven, who saw my faithfulness and my zeal in what He had given me.

To many this work seemed trivial and unrewarding. To me it was a great privilege because I saw it as a work unto my Father. I did it not because I was asked but because I saw that it needed doing. I not only saw the need, but I jumped at the chance to fill it. I saw it as work in His kingdom. I saw it as an opportunity to do a small part in something wonderful. To me it was a job opening! It was as though He had accepted my resume. And I loved making the place comfortable for His people. In that attitude I worked to show myself approved. I worked to become the best janitor in His kingdom. I was at the bottom and enjoying every minute of it.

From sweeping and mopping I was promoted to sweeping, mopping and ushering. From sweeping, mopping, and ushering, I was promoted to sweeping, mopping, ushering and refreshments. To sweeping, mopping, ushering and refreshments was added collections and then opening announcements and then opening prayer and then counseling and then teaching and preaching and so on. And then, in what seemed like a very short while after I picked up that broom and mop, I was a senior pastor.

After more than thirty years in His kingdom I don't get much chance to sweep and mop any more (mainly because those who have heard this story are using all the brooms) but if given a chance to begin again I would go right back to the broom and mop. I learned more about His heart, His kingdom and His nature while I was mopping than at most other times in my life. I spent many fine hours talking to my Father in that place. And in that low place I learned the heart of a servant. In learning that lesson, I learned the foundation for everything I would ever learn about my Lord and my Father – that our Father has a servant's heart.

Just as a farmer's children begin with the basics of farm chores, so do we when we enter the Father's fields at new birth. We are heirs, but we begin by doing the small jobs that no one else wants. How we do them determines the quality of our next job in His house.

Do you want to learn to serve your heavenly Father and really get to know Him? Find the lowest, dirtiest and most unrewarding job you can spot in your church and volunteer to oversee it. Pick the job that no one else wants or offer to help someone who is already laboring in that low place. Volunteer to become deacon of the dust pails or bishop of the boy's room. In that low place you will find your Lord and Father waiting for you. As you begin to serve there in obscurity ask the Lord to teach you about His heart and His ways. I guarantee that you will not be disappointed.

My heavenly Father promoted me naturally. I was never working to be promoted. In fact, I was quite content being a heavenly janitor. He moved me on for the simple reason of supply and demand. True servants are hard to find. Most people serve only to gain the recognition or acceptance of others. True servants, on the other hand, serve only for the pleasure of helping their Father get what He wants. They are their own people. When He finds someone with that type of heart He pours everything He has into their development so that they can do more. The harvest of what He has planted is out there and sincere laborers are so few that true servants must do the work of ten. Those with a pure heart to serve will never remain in the low places for long. They advance quickly.

Advancement in His home and kingdom comes not as a result of academic achievement, but as a reward for faithfulness. To each of us is given a talent. This is a part of His kingdom that He freely gives to us. As free willed children we must choose what to do with those talents. He does not force or manipulate us into using them for His kingdom. We can either choose to invest them in His work or let them lie buried. If we invest the treasure for His good we are rewarded with more. If we bury it we risk losing all.

(the kingdom of heaven is like) a man going on a journey, who called his servants and entrusted his property to them. To one he gave five talents of money, to another two talents, and to another one talent, each according to his

ability. Then he went on his journey. The man who had received the five talents went at once and put his money to work and gained five more. So also, the one with the two talents gained two more. But the man who had received the one talent went off, dug a hole in the ground and hid his master's money. After a long time the master of those servants returned and settled accounts with them. The man who had received the five talents brought the other five. 'Master,' he said, 'you entrusted me with five talents. See, I have gained five more.' His master replied, 'Well done, good and faithful servant! You have been faithful with a few things; I will put you in charge of many things. Come and share your master's happiness!' The man with the two talents also came. 'Master,' he said, 'you entrusted me with two talents; see I have gained two more.' His master replied, 'Well done good and faithful servant! You have been faithful with a few things; I will put you in charge of many things. Come and share your master's happiness!' Then the man who had received the one talent came. 'Master,' he said, 'I knew that you are a hard man, harvesting where you have not sown and gathering where you have not scattered seed. So I was afraid and went out and hid your talent in the ground. See, here is what belongs to you.' His master replied, 'You wicked lazy servant! So you knew that I harvest where I have not sown and gather where I have not scattered seed? Well then, you should have put my money on deposit with the bankers, so that when I returned I would have received it back with interest. Take the talent from him and give it to the one who has the ten talents . . . And throw that worthless servant outside...
Matthew 25:14-30 (NIV)

When we are found trustworthy with smaller matters, we become trusted with more critical matters.

Whosoever can be trusted with very little can also be trusted with much...
Luke 16:10 (NIV)

If you pass up the low place and jump right up to a high place, you can count on ending up back at the low place very soon. No one, and I mean NO ONE, starts at the top and survives. Those who start at the top become top heavy with no foundation and eventually tip over. Secondly, once you find that low place do everything you can to stay in it. If you do this you will be made great, not by men, but by God.

An argument started among the disciples as to which of them would be greatest. Jesus, knowing their thoughts, took a little child and had him stand beside him. Then he said to them, "Whosoever welcomes this little child in my name welcomes me; and whosoever welcomes me welcomes the one who sent me. For he who is least among you all – he is the greatest."
Luke 9:46-48 (NIV)

Jesus is the greatest. He is the greatest because He willingly let Himself be made the lowest on the Cross. He was without any sin and was the Son of the Most High, but He humbly took on the low filthy sin of all men. As a servant to His Father's will, He became a servant to men who did not deserve such love. We can do no less in service to Him.

Our heavenly Father is not a fool and He never wastes true riches. If we hope to move on to bigger and better things, we must begin with the little things that prove our heart. To be trusted with the lives and care of other souls we must be able to be trusted with the simple care of cleaning off seats for them to sit on. If we can't be trusted to accomplish the little services for their care, how can we ever be trusted with matters of eternal life and death?

When we begin in His house He gives us opportunities. These sometimes come in the form of simple requests for help from other servants like setting up chairs or holding a door open. The opportunities begin small. The eye of a true servant is always looking for them and running to be the first to invest their talents. Gradually the opportunities become bigger. Now we've passed the first few tests. Now we can be trusted with more. We go to the next level. From there, opportunities grow in leaps and bounds. Time rushes by and before we know it our talents have been multiplied many times over. The more we give the faster we receive. All the while we are learning about our heavenly Father. Soon we begin to know His heart and then we can begin to hear His voice. Would you like to see Him and hear His voice? It is simple; we learn to hear Him and see Him by being where He is.

Chapter 21

With Him Where He Is

Anyone who wants to be my disciple must follow me, because my servants must be where I am. And the Father will honor anyone who serves me.
John 12:26 (NLT)

When we take a bite out of a big juicy apple, drink a glass of milk or sit down to a steak dinner we are eating the fruit of a farmer's labors. We seldom consider the process that brings these products to our mouth. To us these foods are objects to be consumed for our nourishment and pleasure. To the farmer and his family they are the center of daily life. A farmer has little time to think of much else. Even the training of the farmer's children is intertwined with the daily workload. In other words, the farmer does not train his children by setting up classrooms in the barn. There is simply no time. There are no chalkboard diagrams on how to raise apples. There are no videos to teach the children how to plant and harvest, no textbooks on cow milking, no weekend seminars on leading sheep in the fields, and no Internet connection in the manure shed. Farm children learn by working alongside their father and mother. The work of a farm cannot stop for classes on farming. Until the harvest is completed the work comes first. This learn-as-you-go teaching technique is the best way to learn.

To gain the full heart of our Father and work with Him in His fields we must understand this critical truth: we are not saved to be lazy or selfish. If you have come to salvation in Jesus you already have eternal life and everything you need for life and godliness. Those who have not come to salvation in

Jesus are being held captive to sin and death and are without hope of eternal life. Simply put they do not have the good things you have, and, without your help, they never will.

If this is reality, then how can we focus on anything but the work of giving people what was so freely given to us? With the exception of our personal fellowship with the Father and Son, everything we desire in this life must take second place to that work. When the harvest is completed, at the end of time, we will have plenty of opportunity for celebration and feasting on the good things that came as a result of the good harvest. In this life our joy and pleasure must be centered on producing fruit for His eternal kingdom. Our time here is only temporary and very short. Our true reward comes at the end of our labors. Even though we are already heirs of the promise through Jesus, there is no time to slack off until the race is finished. Until then there is just too much to do. Our Father's greatest pleasure is to fellowship with us, but He has work for us to get done in this age and expects us to do it. He loves us very much, but He also loves those who do not yet know Him. And He expects us to love them too. That is where we are to be today; right there with Him in His labors of love, laboring together with Him until the work of harvest is done.

In this place of service, working alongside Him, investing in His kingdom, we gain opportunity to learn His ways, learn how He thinks, learn what is important to Him, and what He is saying today. In essence, we gain deep knowledge of Him by watching Him work in the lives of others and in our own lives, much the way a farmer's children learn about their father's trade and personal character traits as they live with him and work on his farm.

Consider the learning process that occurs in the growing of just one apple. You may think that the apple began as a seed, but a farmer knows better. In reality the apple began at the farmer's breakfast table long before the seed is planted and the apple reaches your table.

Sitting around the breakfast table each morning a farmer lays out detailed plans for the day to his children. At that table, before the crack of dawn, he gives assignments to each child. One may be given the chores of tilling the ground in preparation for planting, another the planting of the seeds, another the fertilizing and watering and so on. By the time breakfast is done everyone knows his job, cooperation systems are laid out, and goals are defined.

After breakfast the father and children go out to the fields together. He is there and they are with him. They are laborers together. They carry out his work. They carry his yoke doing the work of the farmer's domain. The apple is the fruit of this co-laboring.

Through this co-laboring two other fruits are produced naturally: first the training of the children in the farmer's kingdom and second, the knowledge of the farmer himself. These gains in knowledge and understanding in the children come as a result of serving in the position they were born into.

Skip forward years in time to the same breakfast table where the farmer's children are now near maturity. The conversation process at the table has changed dramatically. No longer does the father need to lay out the day's work in great detail. The matured children have spent so much time working alongside their father that they know his thoughts and concerns for the day. His thoughts, through time, have become their thoughts. His work has become their work. They know what needs to be done on the farm. Through the process of living with and laboring alongside their father, they have entered a new level of communication with him. By serving in obedience during their youth, the children no longer need to be instructed in detail like an employee. They have now come to live and work in the fullness of their father's heritage as a partner with him.

In this mature level of son-ship their fellowship with the father also changes. His passions have become their passions. His glory (reward) has become their reward and whatever the father gains they also gain. They are no longer child-servants, but are now friends of the father. Through service and obedience they have come to inherit more than just the fruits of the father's kingdom. As mature sons and daughters, they also have inherited their father's very nature. In other words, they have become everything that the father is. They have put on his nature. They now possess his knowledge, his wisdom, his authority and his heart in fullness. By gaining this, they have gained all they need for their own lives and have filled their father's heart with the joy of fellowship. By living with him and serving alongside him they have gained all and given him all.

For we are God's fellow workers; you are God's field, God's building.
1 Corinthians 3:9 (NIV)

Our training does not come by sitting in classrooms, reading books or attending seminars. These studies are important for gaining facts and adding to our faith, but alone they leave us incomplete in our knowledge of Him. Our faith - our expression in His life - is perfected and made complete as we do His work;

You foolish man, do you want evidence that faith without deeds is useless? Was not our ancestor Abraham considered righteous for what he did when he offered his son Isaac on the altar? You see that his faith and his

actions were working together, and his faith was made complete by what he did. And the scripture was fulfilled that says, "Abraham believed God, and it was credited to him as righteousness," and he was called God's friend.
James 2:20-23 (NIV)

To see and know the Father is to live with Him and do what He is doing.

Philip said, "Lord, show us the Father, and we will be satisfied." Jesus replied, "Have I been with you all this time, Philip, and yet you still don't know who I am? Anyone who has seen me has seen the Father! So why are you asking me to show him to you? Don't you believe that I am in the Father and the Father is in me? The words I speak are not my own, but my Father who lives in me does his work through me.
John 14:8-10 (NLT)

The disciples lived and served right alongside Jesus through His ministry. In spite of this, it took them years to understand that by being with Jesus wherever He was, and by participating in His work, they were actually coming to know the heavenly Father. Jesus explained, that by the act of being with Him while He did the Father's works, they had actually already seen the Father. Why? Because the Father was there! Jesus knew His Father. The Father was in Jesus. By being where the Father was they had already seen and begun to understand the Father! He was there in Jesus. They were there with Jesus as He worked His Father's will. The Father's works revealed His character and His love. Consequently, they gained the knowledge of their Father by being where He was and doing what He was doing

The disciples were waiting for a giant face to appear in the clouds. They wanted Jesus to open the clouds and let them see the Father. In reality they had already seen the Father and didn't know it. In this life our heavenly Father is easily seen and heard. We need only to go where He is. In this life, He is at work as a shepherd, a farmer and a builder. To see Him and know Him we must go to where His servants are laboring and add our own hands to the labor. To gain His character, we must live in His house, the church. And to hear what He is saying, we must be interested in what He wants to talk about. In this life, He talks about the things a farmer would be discussing around the breakfast table; the day's work.

He is, by His own choice, down in the valleys of humanity working at harvesting as many as will come to Him. He is motivated by His own loving passion to save as many as He can before the appointed end. If you want to be with Him you must go there and work with Him. Take up His yoke and work on His farm doing what He is doing in this age. If you do this, you will know Him. It is that simple. And just as any child of a farmer knows, you will get out of it what you put in.

Chapter 22

Thirty - Sixty - Hundredfold

And these are they which are sown on good ground; such as hear the word, and receive it, and bring forth fruit, some thirtyfold, some sixty, and some an hundred.
Mark 4:20 (KJV)

I had opportunity to employ a variety of folks in the building and remodeling company that I owned. Of the employees who worked productively for me over the years, I was always able to organize them into three basic groups; *those who did what they were told, those who did what they knew to do,* and *those who did whatever needed to be done.*

The first group: *those who did what they were told,* were reliable and executed whatever I asked. But after they accomplished their appointed tasks, they stopped working.

The second group: *those who did what they knew to do,* could be relied on to use their talents to fully accomplish whatever they knew to be their accountability on the project. They worked all day doing whatever they were assigned and doing whatever their job title called for.

The third group: *those who did whatever needed to be done,* not only did what they were told and did the work of their job title, but would also do anything to help get the job done. They would even do other people's work after they had finished with their own. Whether it was a room that needed to be cleaned or a pile of nails that needed boxing, they would accomplish the tasks as they saw them. Without fail these employees were promoted and eventually assumed the role of foremen overseeing others. To these employees, I could entrust a day's work or an entire project without concern over its proper execution. They did the work with a passion as though the company was their own. To be expected these were the ones in whom I personally confided not only as employees, but also as friends. As they invested in my work, I returned the investment by giving them greater knowledge and insight in the trade. Of these almost all went on to own their own businesses or attained greater success in the trades.

In God's kingdom these three groups are referred to as, 30-fold, 60-fold, and 100-fold. Here is the great opportunity offered by His kingdom; we can decide how far we go in His life and how well we grow to know Him.

Some of God's children do only what they are told. These are *30-Fold* children. They are His children. He loves them and they are not condemned for doing only what they are told. But they miss so much. In their lifetime they experience only a third of their Father's glory and they produce and become only a third of what they could do or be. There is no sin in this. They are still better than those who never do anything at all and lose everything, but they miss seventy-percent of knowing their Father.

At the minimum, we are expected to do what we are told. We are expected to obey His words and respond to His call whenever it comes to us. This is the beginning of our faith. This obedience gains us entrance to life in His family.

If a man love me, he will keep my words: and my Father will love him, and we will come unto him, and make our abode with him.
John 14:23 (KJV)

The *60-Fold* child of God not only does what they are told, but they go one step further and do what they know to do.

These children make all of their decisions based on what they know of God's kingdom. They move in reaction to whatever comes their way. When an opportunity is offered to them they quickly volunteer. They serve with great zeal and can be relied on to carry each task and personal challenge to completion. They know a portion of God's ways and serve accordingly. These are content to do one task at a time and feel complete after the task is done. Unfortunately, in their contentment they fail to find the fullness that can be found as a 100-Fold child. They also are His children and are not condemned for missing their full potential. If they would only press on to find the passion of the Father, they could experience and produce so much more.

The ***100-Fold*** child does whatever he or she is told, does everything they know to do, and then goes on to search out and assume accountability for whatever else they find that needs to be done. These serve the Father's kingdom as though it was their very own. They lay down everything of their own lives to be a follower of their Lord and elder brother Jesus. They are busy all the time, but always have time to do one more job for their Father. They serve in zeal and overflowing gladness. No job is too large or too small. They want to see their Father's kingdom grow so much that they are willing to do whatever needs done, whether it be preaching a sermon or cleaning a toilet. They care not about job titles or official roles; they only care about their Father's kingdom going forward. They carry the passion of their Lord. When you talk with them or work alongside them you cannot help but to see the Father in all they do and say. Their spirit is contagious. Their focus is the true love and care of God's children. They sow peace and harvest unity. They fight for what is right with tenacity and believe the best of all. The more they do, the more they are entrusted with. They are promoted rapidly and eventually become the overseers of other's lives as elder Christians. These not only come to know what is expected of them and what to do in His service, but they also know the Father's very heart. They can, at any moment, tell you what the Father is thinking and doing in this day. They know Him intimately by serving so closely at His side. In selfless love they lay down everything for God's work and His children. These are His friends. These are the ones He confides in. In giving up all, these servants gain all. They come to the full knowledge of their Father, prosper well in His life, and have opportunity to fellowship in a fullness that many others miss.

What we do in service to our Father is not as important as how we choose to do it. Our choice reflects our level of faith. It also reflects the depth of our desire to please Him and know Him. Our choice sends a message to our heavenly Father. What we say is never as important as what we do. What we do is the proof, the evidence, of what is really in our heart. Our heavenly Father responds to our level of faith. If we choose to serve Him in the 30-fold realm, He will reveal Himself that way and so forth in the 60 and 100-fold realm choices. By our decisions, we decide ourselves what we get back. This is only right.

The hard-working farmer ought to be the first to receive his share of the crops.
2 Timothy 2:6 (NAS)

A farmer's child who does only what he or she is told to do is serving only like a little child. As soon as the assignment is completed the child sits down in the dirt to play. The sixty fold child does everything he or she knows to do on the farm that is within their accountability and goes back to the house when done. But the hundred-fold child of the farmer will do his own work, the work of the other two and then surveys the entire farm to check for other work that needs done before daylight is gone. Which of the three should receive the most? Which do you think will get to know the Father more?

Do what you are told to do. Do everything you know to do. And, look for anything that needs to be done in His kingdom. Take advantage of each common and divine opportunity in every way. In the end you will be rewarded accordingly. Our service should not be centered on some mystical ministry call. Our own special ministry will be made clear in time after we do everything else that we can find to do now. Chasing after ministries can become a terrible snare. In these days, there are some big time churches built on an amazing variety of ministries for people to get involved in. Setting our sights on a higher calling is not wrong, this is a necessary part of our faith. But to turn away from present opportunities because they do not seem to fit our dream ministry, or because we want the attention of men, will only stunt our growth by robbing us of the simple labors in which we come to know our Father.

Imagine living all of the fullness of your heavenly Father! You can! Just put your hand to His work with everything you are. Give Him 100-percent and watch Him open Himself up to you 100-percent in return.

Chapter 23

Do What He Is Doing

So Jesus explained, "I tell you the truth, the Son can do nothing by himself. He does only what he sees the Father doing. Whatever the Father does, the Son also does.
John 5:19 (NLT)

After a few years of growth, the church that I pastor came to need a larger meeting hall. When choosing a building we made a conscious decision to stay within the boundaries of our local community. Unfortunately, the town is a historic community over a hundred years old with limited real estate adequate for a growing church. But we felt it important as a local church to pursue whatever we could find within the town to enable us to be close to our neighborhoods.

Our search led us to the only building available in town; an old abandoned church sanctuary in the center of the community. The sanctuary was in very bad shape. The wainscot wood trim around the walls was partially destroyed and badly worn. An old automobile transmission was lying in a pool of grease in front of the stage, and all the plaster walls were cracked and peeling. But it was right where we needed it to be in the community.

After a lot of hard work, the old place shaped up very nicely but being a hundred year old wood structure, it still requires a mammoth amount of effort to keep clean every week. Each Saturday morning a crew of church ladies arrive to clean and set up for the Sunday morning services. It takes all morning to get the job done right. They sweep, dust and scrub everything in sight. These women, by their service, make our little old church building livable. By Sunday morning all is well. No one coming to worship needs to worry about sitting on a chair covered with age-old coal dust that still drifts in from the wood ceiling. No one needs to be concerned about the property being ready to receive visitors. The restrooms are sparkling, towels are in the dispenser, floors are clean, supplies are replenished and everything is in order. As a result, everyone who comes can walk right in, sit down, and enjoy the Word of the Lord without thought for those physical needs.

What does this mean to God's kingdom? These ladies, by their faithful service to these general tasks, have made a better place for God's greater works to be accomplished. Every Saturday morning these ladies gather at the side of the Lord and clean house with Him. They do work that is invaluable to the Father's kingdom. In their service they have become an encouragement, have made provision for others, have served others, and are an example for all to follow. The Father's nature is seen clearly in their faithful service.

Where do you think their heavenly Father is on Saturday morning? Right there with them!

If we believe that we are His children, and have come to understand that we learn, grow, and prosper by being at His side, then we must naturally understand that to work with Him means doing whatever He is doing on the earth today, each day, one day at a time. To explain this we can use the example of a farm again.

On a farm there are everyday chores that must be done. Chores such as sweeping out the barns, collecting eggs, feeding the livestock, etc, go on continually every day, year round. There is also seasonal work such as, plowing the fields, planting, weeding, harvesting, nurturing newborn livestock, etc. This work is always in flux and on a good farm becomes

Life With Our Father

more demanding as the farm grows. Everyone on the farm has a job, but basically the children of the farmer do what their father and mother are doing, whether sheering sheep or shoveling manure.

Likewise in our Father's kingdom there are chores needing done. This is the work we do with Him day-after-day, season-after-season through the years. In His faithfulness we can find Him working in these simple places and can jump right in alongside at any time. The daily chores are no less important than the more dramatic seasonal chores. In fact, they are more important in the sense of really getting to know the Father.

Each morning He calls us to these everyday works. We do not need to pray to know this part of His will for us. It is already revealed in His Word. For example we are called to,

> Encourage one another daily, Hebrews 3:13,
> Comfort one another, 1 Thessalonians 4:18,
> Build up & strengthen one another, 1 Thessalonians 5:11,
> Teach and train up one another, Colossians 3:16,
> Provide for one another, Romans 12:13,
> Correct & restore one another, Galatians 6:1,
> Bear one another's burdens, Galatians 6:2,
> Lay down our lives for each other, 1 John 3:16,
> Love one another, 1 Peter 1:22,
> Preach the word, 2 Timothy 4:2,
> Serve one another, Galatians 5:13,
> Be an example to others, 1 Timothy 4:12,
> Pray for one another. James 5:16,

And the list goes on. This is the everyday work of the kingdom. It is our reasonable service to Him. This is the minimum expected of all of us. But in no way is it least in importance to His work. Everyday work is the foundation to greater opportunity.

Let me tell you about a lady I know named Chrissie. Chrissie's works are a good example of laboring honorably in everyday works. Chrissie is a person who is always searching out little jobs that go undone. Literally she fills the gaps in the working of her local church. Chrissie is a constant encouragement by her zealous handling of the little things that hinder the work of the Lord. She is also a very quiet person. She hangs in the background, listens and watches. The moment she sees or hears of a need, she goes right to work. Days or weeks later the need is met with little notice or fanfare. But by her service, the great works go on unhindered. Chrissie is also a door greeter on Sunday mornings. In that position, this quiet woman suddenly turns into a smiling, back slapping, and handshaking encourager. Again she is an encouragement to all. To those looking on from a distance, her service seems small but in reality she sets the tone for the Sunday morning service at the door. A simple example of everyday works, but profound in value to the house of God on the earth today. These are opportunities that every believer can step into. We begin to better understand our Father's ways when we do what He is doing in everyday life.

As noted previously, the more you do the more you will be trusted with. Eventually, in a healthy church, other opportunities of service will open up to you. Answering the call to everyday works and working them faithfully at the Father's side will reveal your talents to others and open the Father's heart to you.

So all of us who have had that veil removed can see and reflect the glory of the Lord. And the Lord - who is the

Spirit - makes us more and more like him as we are changed into his glorious image.
2 Corinthians 3:18 (NLT)

Historically the church has gone through many dramatic divine seasons, or movements. On the surface these movements seem to come and go, thus the title of, *"movement."* But in reality there is always a divine *moving forward* going on in the earth from one glory to another since the beginning. In between each dramatic wave is what seems a quiet time. But the Lord is moving none-the-less supernaturally amongst His church. The time in between is seldom seen as a move of God, simply because there is not a lot of dramatic outward action during these times. But God's movement forward never stops.

One thing we know for sure; we are part of God's glory today, and, we have opportunity to labor in whatever season is yet to come. He is making everything ready in His local churches around the world. He is moving in the hearts and lives of His men and women everywhere, readying them for what is next.

Today, in churches that strive to hear Him and answer His call, there is an intense investment being made into the raising up of that mature corporate child of God. These are a people forging together every part of His church into the image of Jesus. Those who take the time to learn about Him by living with Him and by answering His call to work alongside Him will be those who have a part in this day.

What is the focus of His work? In one word: RESCUE.

The eternal plan of the Father has always been to rescue His creation from eternal separation from His presence. It is the reason Jesus died. All of the general works we are called to are intended to bring many sons and daughters to salvation, so that the Father can be glorified for His goodness and live with us forever.

> *The Lord said, "Say not ye, There are yet four months, and then cometh harvest? Behold I say unto you, Lift up your eyes, and look on the fields; for they are white already to harvest.*
> John 4:35 (KJV)

The Lord of the harvest is always searching for more laborers to help Him with this divine passion to rescue as many as He can.

> *the harvest truly is great, but the laborers are few: pray ye therefore the Lord of the harvest, that he would send forth laborers into his harvest.*
> Luke 10:2 (KJV)

There is a cry coming from the heart of our Father for each of us to rise up and invest what we have into His house and His purposes. I am not just talking about an investment into an organization or system. His church is His people. The investment being called for is one that demands our personal care and service to the lives of those in His house and to those He is calling. That is what it means to rescue someone. It is not enough just to get them in the door of a building we call church. It is more than just teaching Sunday school, shaking a visitor's hand or cleaning a bathroom. This higher investment calls us to a sincere fellowship with every believer in His house and extending that opportunity for fellowship to those who do not know Him. It is about permitting our lives to be part of their lives, and opening our own hearts to receive from others.

This is what it takes to harvest someone for the Lord, to rescue him or her from death.

This is easier said than done. In reality, this means being open to all of the weaknesses of others and being willing to expose our own weaknesses to the same. This is a frightening thing. To be part of this present work we must be willing to get right down on the floor of the sheep barn with everyone else and work our way out together. There is nothing pretty in the sheep barn. It is crowded, wet, dirty and it stinks. But those who decide to tough it out in faith and love will emerge new and strong. In the barn the key words are long-suffering, patience, kindness, gentleness, forgiveness and selflessness.

This is where God is today; right down in the barn birthing the new glories that He has called forth for this age. This is where His servants can be found building up His people to fullness. Through this work, we will become the image of the Lord and thus show forth the Father Himself upon the earth. If you are reading this today, you have a part in this current work. You carry the glory of the Father within you. I encourage you to invest it now into the lives of your brothers and sisters in Christ, so that we can all benefit from your treasures and that you may experience the glory that is unfolding even now.

He desires your help in His fields to rescue His creation from darkness, whether it is in everyday works or the seasonal works of His purposes.

Never fear the work of the Father. His work is never oppressive or impossible. With his power and authority working in you, any task becomes do-able. In fact there is great peace and rest in working alongside the Lord in His fields and great knowledge of God to be gained in the process.

"Come to me, all you who are weary and burdened, and I will give you rest. Take my yoke upon you and learn from me, for I am gentle and humble in heart, and you will find rest for your souls. For my yoke is easy and my burden is light."
Matthew 11:28-30 (NIV)

PART SIX

WITH HIM IN FULLNESS

There is no reason for death to reign any longer. If it does, we cannot blame God. If it is reigning in your own life or the lives of your loved ones, do not blame God. He made a way for it to be put away. The only question remaining is: when will we use what He has given us?

Chapter 24

I Am My Father's Child

"Hello, Smith residence."

"Hello Mr. Smith, this is Bob calling from the Rightway Map Company. We have a special offer to make you on one of our fine maps. The map is..."

"Excuse me, Bob, but my father is not interested."

"Oh, I thought I was talking to the man of the house."

"Bob, I am my father's child, and believe me, he is not interested."

I was sitting in the living room of a church elder's home listening to his son in the other room on the phone. After he hung up, he came into the room and recounted the conversation. Sam, the elder's son, was in his late teens. In his time growing in his father's home, he knew that his dad did not respond to any phone solicitations. He did not need to go to the next room to check. He knew his father's ways. When he was confronted by the salesperson, he simply moved in his father's authority and executed his will. The salesperson had no choice but to bow to Sam's position as his father's son.

This is a good example of the call on our lives as we come to maturity in the knowledge and fellowship of our heavenly Father. As we grow in the knowledge of how He sees things and how He wants things to be, we become able to execute His full will on the earth with authority. The whole of creation is groaning for this amazing unveiling of His sons.

For the anxious longing of the creation waits eagerly for the revealing of the sons of God.

Romans 8:19 (NAS)

Why is creation waiting expectantly for the days when we will be fully matured? Consider verses 20- 21 of Romans 8,

> *But with eager hope, the creation looks forward to the day when it will join God's children in glorious freedom from death and decay.* (NLT)

As matured sons and daughters of God we represent Him. In actuality, we hold His authority from birth in His kingdom, but in our youth we do not know or clearly understand its use. Until Sam matured and came to understand his father's ways he only occupied a place in his father's home. After maturing he not only occupied space, but also now manifested the very desires of his father through his own life. In the home, he was a walking, talking, breathing manifestation of his father's will and authority. And he knew how to use it.

> *After this manner therefore pray ye: Our Father which art in heaven. Hallowed by thy name. Thy kingdom come. Thy will be done IN EARTH, as it is in heaven.*
> Matthew 6:9-10 (KJV)

The Lord instructs us to pray for the Father's will to be done in the earth, the way it is in heaven. How is His will done in heaven? COMPLETELY! Everything there in Heaven is already conformed to His will! His will for the earth is that everything in the earth be completely conformed to His will! What will happen when it all comes into alignment with His will? The earth will be freed from corruption and decay! Can you see now why all of creation longs for the day when this will be completed?

On what does all this hinge? THE REVEALING OF THE SONS OF GOD! The point when you and I come together in the full knowledge of our Father! I have listened in sadness to many men and women who blame God for death and suffering on the earth. They ask why? Why does God permit these things? But even today, as many suffer and die throughout the earth, God has made a way for it all to end. He gave his only Son to die on a cross so that we, all men and women, can be free from the power of sin and death. It is our accountability to accept the freedom and use the authority of the position that salvation brings to us.

There is no reason for death to reign any longer. If it does, we cannot blame God. If it is reigning in your own life or the lives of your loved ones, do not blame God. He made a way for it to be put away. The only question remaining is: when will we use what He has given us?

There is no power that can hold you back. Because of the sacrifice Christ made on that Cross we can walk right into the throne room and ask our Father for anything good. Not even the devil has power over you. The devil has no authority over Jesus. Jesus has prepared you and me to stand up together and declare, "I am my Father's child and this is what *He* says...!"

Why is the earth in such bad shape? The answer is of course the presence of sin and the death that sin produces. Adam, the first man, made a free choice to follow the leading of the devil in the garden. He was not forced. He was not under the power of that serpent. He was created free. He was also created to have dominion over the earth. The earth was under Adam's authority. By choosing the way offered to him by the devil he not only willfully broke fellowship with God, but also opened the door to the death that comes from the ways of darkness. From that simple choice of selfishness, death began to work in the earth through the hearts of men.

Jesus was given all authority at His death and resurrection, and then He gave it to us. The only thing that remains is to destroy the works of the devil. The work of the devil is the bondage and death of mankind. This was Jesus' mission concerning the devil,

> *For this purpose the Son of God was manifested, that he might destroy the works of the devil.*
> 1 John 3:8b (KJV)

We undo the works that the devil has done by declaring light into the darkness. Light drives out darkness. Once the power of the darkness is driven out, healing of its damage can begin. This is our work as His children. We carry His message and His power to push out the enemy and heal the effected soul.

There is a subject in the modern church referred to as, the rapture. Some believe we will fly away out of this mess before it gets too bad. Others believe we will fly away at the start of the end, in the middle of the end, and still others at the end of the end. Whatever your opinion is on this, let me ask this, are we to simply occupy a place, mindlessly packed up and ready to go until He finishes everything, or are we to be using His authority to bring His will in the earth?

> *All power is given unto me in heaven and in earth. Go ye therefore, and teach all nations, baptizing them in the name of the Father, and the Son, and of the Holy Ghost: teaching them to observe all things whatsoever I have commanded you...*
> Matthew 28:18-20 (KJV)

This command from the Gospel of Matthew does not sound like passive occupation to me. This is clearly a command to GO! Notice the first sentence of that great commission which Jesus left us, *"All power is given unto me..."* BUT READ ON, *"Go ye therefore.."* All power was already His! Everything was already under His control! The earth, the devil, mankind, everything! In spite of this, He did not say, "All power has been given unto Me, so now you can just sit around and wait until the end." And He did not say, "All power is given unto Me, so pack your bags and get ready to fly." No! All of the power that He gained was given to us to do His work on the earth. In Heaven, His will is already done! Now it must come to fullness in the earth! His will must be done in the earth, as it is already done in heaven. In heaven everything is bowed down to Jesus. Everything there is living in His glory and power. On the earth this is not yet seen. But before the end it will be so.

> *And this is the plan: At the right time he will bring everything together under the authority of Christ—everything <u>in heaven and on earth</u>.*
> Ephesians 1:10 (NLT)

The end, the completion of His will on this earth, is the end of our work. Our work is to do His full will. His full and complete will is not only our own salvation, but the freedom of all creation as well.

Does this mean we need to demonstrate in front of a sinner's home or business? No! This means that we are to be His sons and daughters! We are to declare the good news that freedom has come by Jesus. We are to declare His ways to the nations. If they choose not to accept them, He will enforce His will Himself. If the map salesman who spoke to Sam that evening in that church leader's house would have ignored Sam's declaration of his father's will and called back again, Sam's father would have set him straight himself. We are not enforcers. We are representatives. This is not the age of the Old Testament law but rather the age of New Testament grace. In the age of the law, God used men and nature to exact His judgments on those who disobeyed His will. In this age of grace all men are free to choose. If they refuse, their judgment is held until the end. We are not called to judge and condemn people for their actions. We are called to declare His will, to stand up for what is right, shed light on darkness and rebuke what is wrong. When we mature to the fullness He has set for us, our declaration of His message will be irresistible.

What do you think would happen if Christians concentrated all of their energies on being filled with the Word and power of God rather than on devising protest schemes? What if they spent weeks in unified prayer for the souls of those they protest? What if they pursued their gentle salvation rather than shouting curses and scriptures at them? What if they just began to declare the life, love and ways of their Father in love - all day - everyday to this world? If just one came to the fullness of being able to say, " I am my Father's child – here is what He says!" There would be no need to protest! And there would be no protest from the hearer, because the hearer would be face to face with the glory of the Lord - and be ready to listen.

We, His children, do not need to concentrate on bringing the *things* of the earth into conformity. If people come into conformity to His will then the things that people control will follow! Mankind is presently using the earth for the fulfillment of sensual desires. This is why all of creation is groaning. Creation is being used today to serve the sin and death of people who are not living in the life of God. We, His children,

His church, must be the standard set for us by Jesus Christ the head of the church.

The scriptures tell us that we are the salt of the earth, the preservative. But when salt has lost its potency it preserves nothing. By opening our hearts to darkness we lose our potency. When the preserving power of the church is lost, everything begins to decay. When a church takes on the spirit of this world it shifts its members away from true life and towards plastic artificial life. Morality and accountability is relaxed. Selfishness then begins to reign as church members seek God for what He can give them rather than what He wants from them. True evangelism based in a personal relationship with the Father and His children is replaced with slick marketing and offers of the Christian high-life. Churches departed into these ways rob the world of God's true salt.

The world needs our salt. Every nation needs our salt. Salt preserves life. If we will rise up as a church and turn back to the face of our Father, He will heal the land. When we rise up He will restore our potency. When the salt is restored to the land, the decay will melt away and restoration will come.

If My people, which are called by My Name, shall humble themselves, and pray, and seek my face, and turn from their wicked ways; then will I hear from heaven, and will forgive their sins, and will heal their land.
2 Chronicles 7:14 (KJV)

You notice in this scripture that He does not say we should be running about the nation judging others or condemning them for their wrongs. Rather we should be judging ourselves and correcting our own course. When this, and only this, happens the land will be healed.

1 John 4 tells us how His love is completed;

No one has ever seen God. But if we love each other, God lives in us, and his love is brought to full expression in us.
1 John 4:12 (NLT)

His love working out of us to others brings His love to completion. It brings His love to completion in us, in our churches, and in the earth.

The Lord says He will pour out His Spirit on all flesh, and all will see it before the end. What will He pour His Spirit from? From you! You are the temple of the Holy Ghost! The Holy Ghost is in you forever! You are the vessel in which His treasure is held! His living waters flow from you,

He that believeth on Me, as the scripture hath said, out of his belly shall flow rivers of living water.
John 7:38 (KJV)

When He pours out His Spirit on all flesh it will indeed be coming from you. You are your Father's child. You are the vessel He will be pouring from. Jesus in you is the light of the world. The completion of His love of the world will be accomplished through you as you abide in Jesus.

All of creation is waiting anxiously for you to go on to perfection in Him, to get to know Him perfectly. It is waiting for the day when you begin to move, speak and live in His authority. To this end, you are being called today. To follow this progression to fullness and perfection is true mature thinking, and mature thinking is what the Father wishes for us. Why? - Because He wants mature children to fellowship with. Wouldn't you? In your pursuit to know your Father be sure to know that to be with Him in fullness means to represent Him in that fullness in this earth. His will is executed in that expression of His character. In that He takes great delight in you and I, and we gain opportunity to know more of Him.

Chapter 25

Manifesting His Glory

When he shall come to be glorified in his saints, and to be admired in all them that believe (because our testimony among you was believed) in that day. That the name of our Lord Jesus Christ may be glorified in you, and ye in him, according to the grace of our God and the Lord Jesus Christ.
2 Thessalonians 1:10, 12 (KJV)

    One of the great joys of being a father to four very active children was to witness their participation and development in academic and extra-curricular activities. However, until I was in the thick of it, I never quite realized the time investment that these activities demand from a parent. By the time our third child was five years old, my wife and I were spending sixteen hours a week running children to and from basketball, football, baseball, ballet, tap and acrobatic activities that involved practices, games and competitions. On top of that I was coaching football and my wife was coaching cheerleading.

    After a couple years of this, I began to wonder if it was worth it all. But one evening at a youth football banquet something occurred that brought it all into focus for me.

    It was my oldest son's first year of peewee football. I was working a job that required me to travel many exhausting city miles per day. My wife also worked and her job often required her to work well into the evening. Circumstances dictated that the accountability of getting our son to and from his daily practice sessions be handled by me. Each day I would rush home from work, grab my son and his equipment and head off to the practice field just barely getting him there in time for the start of practice.

Next to the field was an old maple tree that afforded me a bit of protection from the elements and a place to lean during the two-hour practices. Through sun, rain, wind and snow, throughout the fall football season, I could be found huddled against that tree, still dressed in my business suit.

On more than one occasion, standing there at the mercy of the elements, I wrestled with the value of this investment. Not only were the circumstances less than comfortable, but my son was so small that he rarely got a chance to play. I was more than happy when that season ended.

Several weeks after the season was finished, we arrived with our son at the annual season-end banquet. The event was being held at a local fire hall. As we walked through the front doors my son spied a long folding table covered with shiny gold trophies.

After finding our seats, my son very quietly slipped away to get a closer look at the trophies on that front table. Seconds later he came back to our table with a smile on his little face that stretched from ear to ear. "Dad," he gasped, "My name is on one of those trophies!" After seeing that little trophy he could think of nothing else. Through the meal and the guest speakers, he kept his eyes riveted on that trophy table.

Having been involved in sports in my youth, I understood his fascination and expectation. To me, however, on that night I was enjoying my chicken dinner much more than the thought of him winning that trophy. I was of course happy for him and enjoyed watching him in his excitement and anticipation as he squirmed impatiently waiting for the awards ceremony to begin. And I was full of joy that this would be a special night for him, but I was not prepared for what would happen in my own heart that night.

As the awards ceremony commenced, the young players were called forward one at a time to receive their trophies and shake their coaches' hands. With each name called out over the loudspeaker system, my son slid a bit closer to the edge of his seat. Finally his name was called. Using every bit of self-control he could muster to keep from leaping up and racing forward, he walked the fifty feet to the podium in a half-walk half-run. I was filled with joy for him and began to applaud with everyone else in the room. What happened next I'm sure seemed very insignificant to everyone else in the hall that night, but to me it brought the meaning of my own fatherhood and the fatherhood of God into sharp focus.

As each player received their trophy, they walked down a line made up of their head coach and assistant coaches to shake hands and receive a pat on the back. I watched as my son went from coach to coach shaking hands. As he reached his hand out to the last coach in the line, the man reached over and grabbed the microphone, put his hand on my son's shoulder and said for everyone in the room to hear, "This young man didn't get much of a chance to play this year, but he practiced and played with the heart of someone twice his size." With that he patted him on the back and sent him on his way.

My son was so totally overjoyed with his shiny trophy, I don't think he even heard what the coach had said, but back at the table I was experiencing something that I had never known before.

When the coach said those words I smiled and looked across our table at the people who were sitting with us that night. They were smiling at me and nodding their heads in approval. My son, so small that he had to have a special helmet ordered, only playing in a handful of plays during the season and at the ripe old age of only nine years, had brought me glory. It was overwhelming to my heart.

I never felt this type of joy before that moment. And even though I had won personal awards growing up, none of them brought me the satisfaction and accomplishment this moment brought to me.

By showing up on time, and pouring everything he had into those practices during the season, my young son had achieved recognition for his character. His achievements became glory to both of us. He received glory that night for his attitude and hard work while I received glory for the investment of my time and dedication to raise him up in these attitudes. And it was truly glorious.

This is part of our fellowship with our heavenly Father. This is the glorious reason He had us as children - why you and I were born. We were created to show forth the glories of our Father God. In our achievements, He receives glory. In our successes, He is glorified. When we overcome difficulties, scale a mountain in our life, execute wisdom in our jobs, or train up a godly child, He is recognized and glorified through us now and forever. And He loves it. He glories in the glory that our lives bring Him. He experiences the same type of joy that I experienced that evening with my son. It is a unique kind of unselfish glory that comes as a result of unselfish investment into the life of another, into the life of a child.

This is what our Father is all about. He gives us everything we need to succeed in life. Everything He does for us is completely unselfish. Through the ages He has continually invested everything He has and is into us so that we can succeed and get the ultimate trophy.

At the end of time as we know it, when all the seasons have ended, when each of us goes forward to receive the highest prize in front of all of creation at the biggest banquet of all, He will be glorified in the midst of our moment of glory. At that moment, we will be glorified for running and completing the greatest race of all, and He will be glorified for the training, provision and love that He invested in each of us through the ages.

Even the smallest of our achievements brings glory to Him. Through the years each of my children have brought glory to me in their own way. I learned through my children's lives that it is not the size of the accomplishment that is important, but rather the quality of their attitude and effort that make the successes worthwhile. That is good fruit. When we bear fruit and succeed our heavenly Father is glorified,

Herein is my Father glorified, that we bear much fruit...
John 15:8 (KJV)

When you produce much fruit, you are my true disciples. This brings great glory to my Father.
John 15:8 (NLT)

The word, glorified, here in John 15:8, indicates *the bringing to the light of what is already inside*. The glory of the Father is in us from new birth by the Holy Spirit. The maturing process that brings us to His fullness causes that unseen nature of our Father to be seen by what it produces in our life. When the fruit of what we permit to grow in our lives comes to the surface, everyone will notice and say, "What a great God it is that could do this in a life such as yours." And in that our Father gets the glory.

Imagine millions walking the streets of this world, working in factories, living in neighborhoods, and serving in local churches, with the glory of God flowing out of their lives in this way. Imagine each bearing much fruit for all to see.

What a cloud of glory that would be lifted up to our Father! Look for it! It is coming!

This is the true manifestation of the sons and daughters of God; each bearing much fruit by following the Spirit to complete salvation of the soul and on to perfection. We are called to do this for our Father. He is worthy to be glorified this way.

Consider how much my frail human heart was moved when my son bore fruit to my glory at that football banquet. Now imagine how the heart of our heavenly Father will be moved when an army of His sons and daughters are pouring out fruit all over the earth.

> *"Arise, shine; for your light has come, And the glory of the LORD has risen upon you. "For behold, darkness will cover the earth And deep darkness the peoples; But the LORD will rise upon you And His glory will appear upon you. "Nations will come to your light, And kings to the brightness of your rising.*
> Isaiah 60:1-3 (NAS)

And finally imagine how your heart and life would be overwhelmed by the very presence of your heavenly Father as you walk with Him in such a fashion. Get excited! It is within your grasp.

Chapter 26

Mature Thinking

That I may know Him, and the power of His resurrection and the fellowship of His sufferings, being conformed to His death; in order that I may attain to the resurrection from the dead. Not that I have already obtained it, or have already become perfect, but I press on in order that I may lay hold of that for which also I was laid hold of by Christ Jesus. Brethren, I do not regard myself as having laid hold of it yet; but one thing I do; forgetting what lies behind and reaching forward to what lies ahead, I press on toward the goal for the prize of the upward call of God in Christ Jesus. Let us therefore, as many as are perfect (mature), have this attitude.
Philippians 3:10-15 (NAS)

So where do we go from here? There is so much more!

At new birth into Christianity we are instructed in God's Word to be baptized in water. This water baptism signifies our legal justification before the heavens. This justification is likened to an inmate on death row who is suddenly and freely released from his penalty of death by another dying in his place. This is the debt that Jesus paid for us on the Cross. He died in our place. By His sacrifice our eternal spirit is saved. In this baptism we become God's little children. We are born into our inheritance. This is only the beginning.

The second baptism we are called to is the baptism of the Holy Ghost,

> *When the apostles in Jerusalem heard that Samaria had accepted the word of God, they sent Peter and John to them. When they arrived, they prayed for them that they might receive the Holy Spirit, because the Holy Spirit had not yet come upon any of them; they had simply been baptized into the name of the Lord Jesus. Then Peter and John placed their hands on them, and they received the Holy Ghost.*
> Acts 8:14-17 (NIV)

In the first baptism, we are born of the Spirit, John 3:5. In the second baptism, we are filled with His Spirit. (As seen in the case of the new believers at Samaria.) This filling brings to us the indwelling power of our God. This indwelling Spirit of God leads us progressively through the sanctification of our souls. Sanctification simply means separation from one place to another. This is the work of the Spirit teaching us about God's Word, leading us through tribulation, etc. This also works in us through chastisements and in our relationships with other Christians in His church. Through it all we are progressively separated from the old ways of thinking and living and brought to new ways of thinking and living as His children.

This second baptism takes us from the starting place of being saved in our spirits to the process of being saved in our souls. (the soul being our intellect, will and emotions)

> *So get rid of all the filth and evil in your lives, and humbly accept the word God has planted in your hearts, for it has the power to save your souls.*
> James 1:21 (NLT)

In this process of putting off the old ways and putting on His ways, we come to learn about Him and to know Him much deeper. This is the sanctifying work of the Holy Spirit in God's children and His church today. This work is an ongoing process.

This is all good – but it is not *all*.

forgetting those things which are behind, and reaching forth unto those things which are before, I press toward the mark for the prize of the high calling of God in Christ Jesus.
Philippians 3:13b-14 (KJV)

When Paul was writing to the Philippians there in chapter 3, he was already baptized in the water and in the Spirit (Acts 9:17-18) If this was the end of his pursuit, what was he saying when he said that he *was pressing on to the goal of the higher prize*? Paul was mature. He had passed through common salvation. What was left? What was he looking forward to and reaching for? It couldn't have been eternal life – he already had it by the justification of Jesus. It couldn't have been sanctification – he had that by faithfully obeying the teaching of the Holy Spirit through his new life. If anyone was ever sanctified, it was Paul.

After justification and after sanctification, comes the third baptism, the baptism of the fire of the Holy Spirit, which is, perfection. Perfection is simply being like our heavenly Father. Everything else along the way is only intended to bring us to perfection. The gifts and ministries brought to us by the church are only temporary until the people of God reach perfection. They are not meant as the end, but as the means to bring us to the end goals that Paul spoke of,

> *He gave some as apostles, and some as prophets, and some as evangelists, and some as pastors and teachers, FOR the equipping of the saints for the work of service to the building up of the body of Christ; UNTIL we all attain to the unity of the faith, and of the knowledge of the Son of God, to a mature man, to the measure of the stature which belongs to the fullness of Christ.*
> Ephesians 4:11-13 (NAS)

Everything that the church has experienced and learned from its beginning until now has been working to bring His people together in unity and knowledge to the fullness of maturity, to perfection. This is not something that will occur only after we are all dead and gone to glory – this will be seen in the earth! If not today, very soon.

I have often told the people I pastor that my greatest accountability as their pastor is to work myself out of a job. Literally my job as a pastor is to equip them well enough that they do not need an earthly pastor. This is how every five-fold minister should be thinking and working. We should be investing everything we are into His children to ensure that they all reach that goal which Paul spoke of, the high call of attaining full maturity to the very image of Jesus.

When we all come together in the unity of the knowledge of Jesus and His image, we will reveal the Fatherhood of our God to every corner of the earth. The power of this matured corporate man will be irresistible. In this we will not only see the things of God and the power of God, but we will see the very person of our Father and Lord revealed before all flesh. When Jesus is lifted up before all the earth in this way, there will come a harvest of souls as never seen before. This is the heritage of those who follow the progression of the Holy Ghost in these last days.

In all of this, the greatest desire of our Father will come to its completion; the fellowship of fully matured children. This is the prize of the upward call that Paul spoke of. This is where we are called to be from the very beginning of our salvation. This is the place that Jesus opened up to us; to be seated right with Him,

> *Even when we were dead in sins, hath quickened us together with Christ, (by grace ye are saved) And hath raised us up together, and made us sit together in heavenly places in Christ Jesus.*
> Ephesians 2:5-6 (KJV)

The New American Standard version reads:

> *...and raised us up with Him, and <u>seated us with Him</u> in the heavenly places in Christ Jesus,*

Our Father loves to cuddle us when we are little children, and He loves to teach us as young men and women. But more than anything, He waits for the fellowship that comes when we become fully grown. Everything through history up until now is working to that purpose.

The scriptures tell us that in the last days this work will dramatically speed up and the days will be shortened. Look about you. This has been evident since the turn of the last century and even more so into this new century. And it is even more evident as each day passes. We are all rushing to perfection. Do not look to the old days to compare the passing of spiritual time. There are no days that have been like the days we are in now. The Father wants His mature children and He is quickening everything and everyone to get them.

The Better Life of Knowing God

The time has come to move on from the foundational doctrines to the completion of the building and on to perfection. It is time to look into the face of the Father rather than just the seeking of His hand and His voice. Deep is calling unto deep. And all of creation is groaning with desire for the manifestation of the mature sons of God.

> *For I, reckon that the sufferings of this present time are not worthy to be compared with the glory which shall be revealed in us. For the earnest expectation of the creature waiteth for the manifestation (revealing) of the sons of God.*
> Romans 8:18-19 (KJV)

This is your invitation from your heavenly Father. Get up. Rise up. Throw yourself into His life. Open His Word, the Bible. Get into the Lord's house. Listen to His Spirit. Learn of His ways. Sit down in the throne room. Take your place created for you by Jesus. Come to the Father. He waits now with open arms to carry you on to the better life He has prepared for you.

PART SEVEN

CONCLUSION

Jesus: the Beginning and the End

He came to the earth as a man for us. He walked to the Cross for us. He took our sins on Himself. He permitted Himself to be mocked and humiliated for us. He gave His blood for us. He rose again for us. He sat down at the right hand of the Father for us. He prepared a place for us. He opened His very own throne seat for us to sit with Him there with the Father.

Chapter 27

We Owe it All to Him

through Him we both have access by one Spirit unto the Father. Ephesians 2:18 (KJV)

I don't recall much about the lost late-teenage years of my life. I was in complete rebellion; staying out till well after midnight, getting into things no teenager should touch, and a dedicated member of a small-town street gang. But I will never forget my mom standing at the kitchen stove stirring her tiny pots of food. That is where I found her every time I dragged my miserable butt into the house after a night of running the streets. There she would be just standing, quietly stirring a pot in her tattered nightgown. Being virtually unconscious at that time in my life, it never really dawned on me why she was up at 1 a.m. cooking. But today I understand. She was there praying for me, waiting for her baby to come home. And every time I came in the door she would quietly talk to me about how special God made me and how wonderful my heavenly Father was.

The darkness of the sixties and seventies seemed to catch her generation unprepared when it came to covering children from danger. Times changed so very rapidly that an entire generation was swept up into all sorts of darkness foreign to her generation. Drugs and sex exploded onto the scene and my parents, like many others of her generation, just had no idea how to deal with it. But my mom went to exactly the right person for help. She took me right to the feet of Jesus.

Every night for months and months my little four-foot-ten-inch tall mom would be waiting for me to tell me about this Jesus. I listened quietly. And then, quietly, slowly, something started to happen in my heart. Everywhere I went I began to hear her soft words reminding of Him. I started to wonder about this fellow Jesus. One night I snuck a Bible into my room and began to read it secretly. I read it every evening for weeks. And each night before slipping off to sleep I would carefully hide it under my mattress to not be discovered. Many weeks passed, and night-by-night God's word started to literally jump off the pages to me. Finally, late one night I just began to weep on my bed. I flicked on the TV and an evangelist just happened to be talking about coming home to the Lord. I fell to my knees right there in my bedroom and laid it all in front of the throne at the feet of my Jesus. And right there on that floor, the man I once was - was buried. My journey into my Father's heart began.

Our conclusion brings us to the beginning.

In the beginning was the Word, and the Word was with God, and the Word was God...All things were made by Him; and without Him was not any thing made that was made. In Him was life; and the life was the light of men...as many as received Him, to them gave He power to become the sons of God, even to them that believe on His name...
John 1:1,3,4,12 (KJV)

All of the good things about our Father that we covered in this book came by Jesus, the Word. Everything the Father gives us comes through Him and everything good that we become during our lives goes back to Him. We owe it all to Jesus Christ the Son of God, the living Word of God.

Jesus willingly gave His own life on the Cross so that:

Through His blood we are redeemed and forgiven... (Colossians 1:14, 1 Peter 1:18-19)
...so that we can be with our heavenly Father today and forever.

Through Him we are free from the power of evil...(Hebrews 2:14, Romans 6:14)
...so that now we can freely choose life with our Father rather than death from sin.

Through Him we can enter the holy of holies in boldness without fear...(Hebrews 10:19-20)
...so that now we can go to, and fellowship with, our Father anytime.

Through Him we have an advocate, one who pleads and intercedes for us, before the Father...(I John 2:1, Romans 8:34)
...so that we do not need to plead in weaknesses for ourselves.

By Him we have obtained God's grace, (free unearned favor)...(Romans 5:15)
...so that we can go on to be mature children of our Father.

In Him we have power and authority to overcome evil on the earth and do His works...(Luke 10:19, Matthew 28:18-20)
...so that we can take part in the work of our Father in this hour.

Everything is by Him. Everything is through Him, and everything is subject to Him. Everything you have read about in this book about your heavenly Father's love is gained through Jesus Christ. Everything concerning your schooling, your service to the Father's kingdom and your membership in His house is by and through Christ Jesus. The Spirit that lives in you today is given to you through Jesus. Every moment of fellowship with the Father that you have enjoyed, you are enjoying now and will enjoy through eternity, are because of Jesus. He came to the earth as a man for us. He walked to the Cross for us. He took our sins on Himself. He permitted Himself to be mocked and humiliated for us. He gave His blood for us. He rose again for us. He sat down at the right hand of the Father for us. He prepared a place for us. He opened His very own throne seat for us to sit with Him there with the Father.

He protects us today. He teaches us, guides us as a shepherd, heals us, and picks us up when we stumble. He is our peace, our counselor, our high priest, our foundation, our light, our daily bread, our Lord the head of the church and our friend.

We owe it all to Jesus. He loves us with a love that is beyond our imagination. He is truly everything to those who are the sons and daughters of the Father. He gave up everything on that Cross, so that the Father could have His desire of being with you and me. And in doing so He gained us as brethren. He is our elder brother. To Him be all glory and dominion forever.

For everything comes from him and exists by his power and is intended for his glory. All glory to him forever! Amen.
Romans 11:36 (NLT)

All thanksgiving and praise to Him. Child of God, when you rise in the morning, give thanks to Him for what He has done. When you are moving through the day, meditate on what He has given you. When you sit down to break bread, remember the sacrifice of the Cross that made your life possible. When you go off to bed, praise Him for His love for you. Never stop. He deserves this and much, much, more. Because of Him, you are a child of the Most High God. Because of Him we can sit and talk to the all-powerful God as our Father. By Him you can really know your heavenly Father. Because of Him, you have fellowship with your Father and will live with Him forever. Because of Him, we never need fear the storms of life. Because of Jesus we have...

...Life With Our Father

Life With Our Father
The Better Life of Knowing God
by James E. Laero

May I never boast except in the cross of our Lord Jesus Christ...
Galatians 6:14 (NIV)

About the Author

Author, James E. Laero, the father of four and grandfather of seven, lives and ministers in the Alle-Kiski Valley region just east of Pittsburgh, Pennsylvania. Through thirty-five years of service to the Lord, he founded more than a dozen ministries impacting people regionally and around the world. Several of these ministries were early pioneer works integrating new technologies and Internet capabilities to publish the Gospel.

Contacts

Web site:
www.lifewithourfather.com

Author's e-mail address:
author@lifewithourfather.com

CPSIA information can be obtained at www.ICGtesting.com
Printed in the USA
LVOW011825161011

250720LV00006B/7/P